C-569

CAREER EXAMINATION SERIES

THIS IS YOUR **PASSBOOK**® FOR ...

SENIOR REAL ESTATE APPRAISER

NATIONAL LEARNING CORPORATION®
passbooks.com

COPYRIGHT NOTICE

This book is SOLELY intended for, is sold ONLY to, and its use is RESTRICTED to individual, bona fide applicants or candidates who qualify by virtue of having seriously filed applications for appropriate license, certificate, professional and/or promotional advancement, higher school matriculation, scholarship, or other legitimate requirements of educational and/or governmental authorities.

This book is NOT intended for use, class instruction, tutoring, training, duplication, copying, reprinting, excerption, or adaptation, etc., by:

1) Other publishers
2) Proprietors and/or Instructors of «Coaching» and/or Preparatory Courses
3) Personnel and/or Training Divisions of commercial, industrial, and governmental organizations
4) Schools, colleges, or universities and/or their departments and staffs, including teachers and other personnel
5) Testing Agencies or Bureaus
6) Study groups which seek by the purchase of a single volume to copy and/or duplicate and/or adapt this material for use by the group as a whole without having purchased individual volumes for each of the members of the group
7) Et al.

Such persons would be in violation of appropriate Federal and State statutes.

PROVISION OF LICENSING AGREEMENTS. — Recognized educational, commercial, industrial, and governmental institutions and organizations, and others legitimately engaged in educational pursuits, including training, testing, and measurement activities, may address request for a licensing agreement to the copyright owners, who will determine whether, and under what conditions, including fees and charges, the materials in this book may be used them. In other words, a licensing facility exists for the legitimate use of the material in this book on other than an individual basis. However, it is asseverated and affirmed here that the material in this book CANNOT be used without the receipt of the express permission of such a licensing agreement from the Publishers. Inquiries re licensing should be addressed to the company, attention rights and permissions department.

All rights reserved, including the right of reproduction in whole or in part, in any form or by any means, electronic or mechanical, including photocopying, recording, or by any information storage and retrieval system, without permission in writing from the Publisher.

Copyright © 2020 by

National Learning Corporation

212 Michael Drive, Syosset, NY 11791
(516) 921-8888 • www.passbooks.com
E-mail: info@passbooks.com

PUBLISHED IN THE UNITED STATES OF AMERICA

PASSBOOK® SERIES

THE *PASSBOOK® SERIES* has been created to prepare applicants and candidates for the ultimate academic battlefield – the examination room.

At some time in our lives, each and every one of us may be required to take an examination – for validation, matriculation, admission, qualification, registration, certification, or licensure.

Based on the assumption that every applicant or candidate has met the basic formal educational standards, has taken the required number of courses, and read the necessary texts, the *PASSBOOK® SERIES* furnishes the one special preparation which may assure passing with confidence, instead of failing with insecurity. Examination questions – together with answers – are furnished as the basic vehicle for study so that the mysteries of the examination and its compounding difficulties may be eliminated or diminished by a sure method.

This book is meant to help you pass your examination provided that you qualify and are serious in your objective.

The entire field is reviewed through the huge store of content information which is succinctly presented through a provocative and challenging approach – the question-and-answer method.

A climate of success is established by furnishing the correct answers at the end of each test.

You soon learn to recognize types of questions, forms of questions, and patterns of questioning. You may even begin to anticipate expected outcomes.

You perceive that many questions are repeated or adapted so that you can gain acute insights, which may enable you to score many sure points.

You learn how to confront new questions, or types of questions, and to attack them confidently and work out the correct answers.

You note objectives and emphases, and recognize pitfalls and dangers, so that you may make positive educational adjustments.

Moreover, you are kept fully informed in relation to new concepts, methods, practices, and directions in the field.

You discover that you arre actually taking the examination all the time: you are preparing for the examination by "taking" an examination, not by reading extraneous and/or supererogatory textbooks.

In short, this PASSBOOK®, used directedly, should be an important factor in helping you to pass your test.

SENIOR REAL ESTATE APPRAISER

DUTIES
Senior Real Estate Appraisers under the direction and supervision of an Associate-level employee, perform a variety of functions including regional field crew supervision, commercial property data collection, and field review of complex properties, valuation modeling, or other related areas.

SUBJECT OF EXAMINATION
Written test designed to test for knowledge, skills, and/or abilities in such areas as:
1. Data collection, including the variables that are collected for residential, commercial, vacant and farm properties for determining values;
2. Applying equalization rates and assessment procedures;
3. Preparing computer inputs and analyzing computer outputs;
4. Preparing written material; and
5. Supervision.

HOW TO TAKE A TEST

I. YOU MUST PASS AN EXAMINATION

A. WHAT EVERY CANDIDATE SHOULD KNOW

Examination applicants often ask us for help in preparing for the written test. What can I study in advance? What kinds of questions will be asked? How will the test be given? How will the papers be graded?

As an applicant for a civil service examination, you may be wondering about some of these things. Our purpose here is to suggest effective methods of advance study and to describe civil service examinations.

Your chances for success on this examination can be increased if you know how to prepare. Those "pre-examination jitters" can be reduced if you know what to expect. You can even experience an adventure in good citizenship if you know why civil service exams are given.

B. WHY ARE CIVIL SERVICE EXAMINATIONS GIVEN?

Civil service examinations are important to you in two ways. As a citizen, you want public jobs filled by employees who know how to do their work. As a job seeker, you want a fair chance to compete for that job on an equal footing with other candidates. The best-known means of accomplishing this two-fold goal is the competitive examination.

Exams are widely publicized throughout the nation. They may be administered for jobs in federal, state, city, municipal, town or village governments or agencies.

Any citizen may apply, with some limitations, such as the age or residence of applicants. Your experience and education may be reviewed to see whether you meet the requirements for the particular examination. When these requirements exist, they are reasonable and applied consistently to all applicants. Thus, a competitive examination may cause you some uneasiness now, but it is your privilege and safeguard.

C. HOW ARE CIVIL SERVICE EXAMS DEVELOPED?

Examinations are carefully written by trained technicians who are specialists in the field known as "psychological measurement," in consultation with recognized authorities in the field of work that the test will cover. These experts recommend the subject matter areas or skills to be tested; only those knowledges or skills important to your success on the job are included. The most reliable books and source materials available are used as references. Together, the experts and technicians judge the difficulty level of the questions.

Test technicians know how to phrase questions so that the problem is clearly stated. Their ethics do not permit "trick" or "catch" questions. Questions may have been tried out on sample groups, or subjected to statistical analysis, to determine their usefulness.

Written tests are often used in combination with performance tests, ratings of training and experience, and oral interviews. All of these measures combine to form the best-known means of finding the right person for the right job.

II. HOW TO PASS THE WRITTEN TEST

A. NATURE OF THE EXAMINATION

To prepare intelligently for civil service examinations, you should know how they differ from school examinations you have taken. In school you were assigned certain definite pages to read or subjects to cover. The examination questions were quite detailed and usually emphasized memory. Civil service exams, on the other hand, try to discover your present ability to perform the duties of a position, plus your potentiality to learn these duties. In other words, a civil service exam attempts to predict how successful you will be. Questions cover such a broad area that they cannot be as minute and detailed as school exam questions.

In the public service similar kinds of work, or positions, are grouped together in one "class." This process is known as *position-classification*. All the positions in a class are paid according to the salary range for that class. One class title covers all of these positions, and they are all tested by the same examination.

B. FOUR BASIC STEPS

1) Study the announcement

How, then, can you know what subjects to study? Our best answer is: "Learn as much as possible about the class of positions for which you've applied." The exam will test the knowledge, skills and abilities needed to do the work.

Your most valuable source of information about the position you want is the official exam announcement. This announcement lists the training and experience qualifications. Check these standards and apply only if you come reasonably close to meeting them.

The brief description of the position in the examination announcement offers some clues to the subjects which will be tested. Think about the job itself. Review the duties in your mind. Can you perform them, or are there some in which you are rusty? Fill in the blank spots in your preparation.

Many jurisdictions preview the written test in the exam announcement by including a section called "Knowledge and Abilities Required," "Scope of the Examination," or some similar heading. Here you will find out specifically what fields will be tested.

2) Review your own background

Once you learn in general what the position is all about, and what you need to know to do the work, ask yourself which subjects you already know fairly well and which need improvement. You may wonder whether to concentrate on improving your strong areas or on building some background in your fields of weakness. When the announcement has specified "some knowledge" or "considerable knowledge," or has used adjectives like "beginning principles of…" or "advanced … methods," you can get a clue as to the number and difficulty of questions to be asked in any given field. More questions, and hence broader coverage, would be included for those subjects which are more important in the work. Now weigh your strengths and weaknesses against the job requirements and prepare accordingly.

3) Determine the level of the position

Another way to tell how intensively you should prepare is to understand the level of the job for which you are applying. Is it the entering level? In other words, is this the position in which beginners in a field of work are hired? Or is it an intermediate or advanced level? Sometimes this is indicated by such words as "Junior" or "Senior" in the class title. Other jurisdictions use Roman numerals to designate the level – Clerk I, Clerk II, for example. The word "Supervisor" sometimes appears in the title. If the level is not indicated by the title, check the description of duties. Will you be working under very close supervision, or will you have responsibility for independent decisions in this work?

4) Choose appropriate study materials

Now that you know the subjects to be examined and the relative amount of each subject to be covered, you can choose suitable study materials. For beginning level jobs, or even advanced ones, if you have a pronounced weakness in some aspect of your training, read a modern, standard textbook in that field. Be sure it is up to date and has general coverage. Such books are normally available at your library, and the librarian will be glad to help you locate one. For entry-level positions, questions of appropriate difficulty are chosen – neither highly advanced questions, nor those too simple. Such questions require careful thought but not advanced training.

If the position for which you are applying is technical or advanced, you will read more advanced, specialized material. If you are already familiar with the basic principles of your field, elementary textbooks would waste your time. Concentrate on advanced textbooks and technical periodicals. Think through the concepts and review difficult problems in your field.

These are all general sources. You can get more ideas on your own initiative, following these leads. For example, training manuals and publications of the government agency which employs workers in your field can be useful, particularly for technical and professional positions. A letter or visit to the government department involved may result in more specific study suggestions, and certainly will provide you with a more definite idea of the exact nature of the position you are seeking.

III. KINDS OF TESTS

Tests are used for purposes other than measuring knowledge and ability to perform specified duties. For some positions, it is equally important to test ability to make adjustments to new situations or to profit from training. In others, basic mental abilities not dependent on information are essential. Questions which test these things may not appear as pertinent to the duties of the position as those which test for knowledge and information. Yet they are often highly important parts of a fair examination. For very general questions, it is almost impossible to help you direct your study efforts. What we can do is to point out some of the more common of these general abilities needed in public service positions and describe some typical questions.

1) General information

Broad, general information has been found useful for predicting job success in some kinds of work. This is tested in a variety of ways, from vocabulary lists to questions about current events. Basic background in some field of work, such as sociology or economics, may be sampled in a group of questions. Often these are principles which have become familiar to most persons through exposure rather than through formal training. It is difficult to advise you how to study for these questions; being alert to the world around you is our best suggestion.

2) Verbal ability

An example of an ability needed in many positions is verbal or language ability. Verbal ability is, in brief, the ability to use and understand words. Vocabulary and grammar tests are typical measures of this ability. Reading comprehension or paragraph interpretation questions are common in many kinds of civil service tests. You are given a paragraph of written material and asked to find its central meaning.

3) Numerical ability

Number skills can be tested by the familiar arithmetic problem, by checking paired lists of numbers to see which are alike and which are different, or by interpreting charts and graphs. In the latter test, a graph may be printed in the test booklet which you are asked to use as the basis for answering questions.

4) Observation

A popular test for law-enforcement positions is the observation test. A picture is shown to you for several minutes, then taken away. Questions about the picture test your ability to observe both details and larger elements.

5) Following directions

In many positions in the public service, the employee must be able to carry out written instructions dependably and accurately. You may be given a chart with several columns, each column listing a variety of information. The questions require you to carry out directions involving the information given in the chart.

6) Skills and aptitudes

Performance tests effectively measure some manual skills and aptitudes. When the skill is one in which you are trained, such as typing or shorthand, you can practice. These tests are often very much like those given in business school or high school courses. For many of the other skills and aptitudes, however, no short-time preparation can be made. Skills and abilities natural to you or that you have developed throughout your lifetime are being tested.

Many of the general questions just described provide all the data needed to answer the questions and ask you to use your reasoning ability to find the answers. Your best preparation for these tests, as well as for tests of facts and ideas, is to be at your physical and mental best. You, no doubt, have your own methods of getting into an exam-taking mood and keeping "in shape." The next section lists some ideas on this subject.

IV. KINDS OF QUESTIONS

Only rarely is the "essay" question, which you answer in narrative form, used in civil service tests. Civil service tests are usually of the short-answer type. Full instructions for answering these questions will be given to you at the examination. But in case this is your first experience with short-answer questions and separate answer sheets, here is what you need to know:

1) Multiple-choice Questions

Most popular of the short-answer questions is the "multiple choice" or "best answer" question. It can be used, for example, to test for factual knowledge, ability to solve problems or judgment in meeting situations found at work.

A multiple-choice question is normally one of three types—
- It can begin with an incomplete statement followed by several possible endings. You are to find the one ending which *best* completes the statement, although some of the others may not be entirely wrong.
- It can also be a complete statement in the form of a question which is answered by choosing one of the statements listed.
- It can be in the form of a problem – again you select the best answer.

Here is an example of a multiple-choice question with a discussion which should give you some clues as to the method for choosing the right answer:

When an employee has a complaint about his assignment, the action which will *best* help him overcome his difficulty is to
- A. discuss his difficulty with his coworkers
- B. take the problem to the head of the organization
- C. take the problem to the person who gave him the assignment
- D. say nothing to anyone about his complaint

In answering this question, you should study each of the choices to find which is best. Consider choice "A" – Certainly an employee may discuss his complaint with fellow employees, but no change or improvement can result, and the complaint remains unresolved. Choice "B" is a poor choice since the head of the organization probably does not know what assignment you have been given, and taking your problem to him is known as "going over the head" of the supervisor. The supervisor, or person who made the assignment, is the person who can clarify it or correct any injustice. Choice "C" is, therefore, correct. To say nothing, as in choice "D," is unwise. Supervisors have and interest in knowing the problems employees are facing, and the employee is seeking a solution to his problem.

2) True/False Questions

The "true/false" or "right/wrong" form of question is sometimes used. Here a complete statement is given. Your job is to decide whether the statement is right or wrong.

SAMPLE: A roaming cell-phone call to a nearby city costs less than a non-roaming call to a distant city.

This statement is wrong, or false, since roaming calls are more expensive.

This is not a complete list of all possible question forms, although most of the others are variations of these common types. You will always get complete directions for answering questions. Be sure you understand *how* to mark your answers – ask questions until you do.

V. RECORDING YOUR ANSWERS

Computer terminals are used more and more today for many different kinds of exams.

For an examination with very few applicants, you may be told to record your answers in the test booklet itself. Separate answer sheets are much more common. If this separate answer sheet is to be scored by machine – and this is often the case – it is highly important that you mark your answers correctly in order to get credit.

An electronic scoring machine is often used in civil service offices because of the speed with which papers can be scored. Machine-scored answer sheets must be marked with a pencil, which will be given to you. This pencil has a high graphite content which responds to the electronic scoring machine. As a matter of fact, stray dots may register as answers, so do not let your pencil rest on the answer sheet while you are pondering the correct answer. Also, if your pencil lead breaks or is otherwise defective, ask for another.

Since the answer sheet will be dropped in a slot in the scoring machine, be careful not to bend the corners or get the paper crumpled.

The answer sheet normally has five vertical columns of numbers, with 30 numbers to a column. These numbers correspond to the question numbers in your test booklet. After each number, going across the page are four or five pairs of dotted lines. These short dotted lines have small letters or numbers above them. The first two pairs may also have a "T" or "F" above the letters. This indicates that the first two pairs only are to be used if the questions are of the true-false type. If the questions are multiple choice, disregard the "T" and "F" and pay attention only to the small letters or numbers.

Answer your questions in the manner of the sample that follows:

32. The largest city in the United States is
    A. Washington, D.C.
    B. New York City
    C. Chicago
    D. Detroit
    E. San Francisco

1) Choose the answer you think is best. (New York City is the largest, so "B" is correct.)
2) Find the row of dotted lines numbered the same as the question you are answering. (Find row number 32)
3) Find the pair of dotted lines corresponding to the answer. (Find the pair of lines under the mark "B.")
4) Make a solid black mark between the dotted lines.

VI. BEFORE THE TEST

Common sense will help you find procedures to follow to get ready for an examination. Too many of us, however, overlook these sensible measures. Indeed, nervousness and fatigue have been found to be the most serious reasons why applicants fail to do their best on civil service tests. Here is a list of reminders:

- Begin your preparation early – Don't wait until the last minute to go scurrying around for books and materials or to find out what the position is all about.
- Prepare continuously – An hour a night for a week is better than an all-night cram session. This has been definitely established. What is more, a night a week for a month will return better dividends than crowding your study into a shorter period of time.
- Locate the place of the exam – You have been sent a notice telling you when and where to report for the examination. If the location is in a different town or otherwise unfamiliar to you, it would be well to inquire the best route and learn something about the building.
- Relax the night before the test – Allow your mind to rest. Do not study at all that night. Plan some mild recreation or diversion; then go to bed early and get a good night's sleep.
- Get up early enough to make a leisurely trip to the place for the test – This way unforeseen events, traffic snarls, unfamiliar buildings, etc. will not upset you.
- Dress comfortably – A written test is not a fashion show. You will be known by number and not by name, so wear something comfortable.
- Leave excess paraphernalia at home – Shopping bags and odd bundles will get in your way. You need bring only the items mentioned in the official notice you received; usually everything you need is provided. Do not bring reference books to the exam. They will only confuse those last minutes and be taken away from you when in the test room.
- Arrive somewhat ahead of time – If because of transportation schedules you must get there very early, bring a newspaper or magazine to take your mind off yourself while waiting.
- Locate the examination room – When you have found the proper room, you will be directed to the seat or part of the room where you will sit. Sometimes you are given a sheet of instructions to read while you are waiting. Do not fill out any forms until you are told to do so; just read them and be prepared
- Relax and prepare to listen to the instructions
- If you have any physical problem that may keep you from doing your best, be sure to tell the test administrator. If you are sick or in poor health, you really cannot do your best on the exam. You can come back and take the test some other time.

VII. AT THE TEST

The day of the test is here and you have the test booklet in your hand. The temptation to get going is very strong. Caution! There is more to success than knowing the right answers. You must know how to identify your papers and understand variations in the type of short-answer question used in this particular examination. Follow these suggestions for maximum results from your efforts:

1) Cooperate with the monitor

The test administrator has a duty to create a situation in which you can be as much at ease as possible. He will give instructions, tell you when to begin, check to see that you are marking your answer sheet correctly, and so on. He is not there to guard you, although he will see that your competitors do not take unfair advantage. He wants to help you do your best.

2) Listen to all instructions

Don't jump the gun! Wait until you understand all directions. In most civil service tests you get more time than you need to answer the questions. So don't be in a hurry. Read each word of instructions until you clearly understand the meaning. Study the examples, listen to all announcements and follow directions. Ask questions if you do not understand what to do.

3) Identify your papers

Civil service exams are usually identified by number only. You will be assigned a number; you must not put your name on your test papers. Be sure to copy your number correctly. Since more than one exam may be given, copy your exact examination title.

4) Plan your time

Unless you are told that a test is a "speed" or "rate of work" test, speed itself is usually not important. Time enough to answer all the questions will be provided, but this does not mean that you have all day. An overall time limit has been set. Divide the total time (in minutes) by the number of questions to determine the approximate time you have for each question.

5) Do not linger over difficult questions

If you come across a difficult question, mark it with a paper clip (useful to have along) and come back to it when you have been through the booklet. One caution if you do this – be sure to skip a number on your answer sheet as well. Check often to be sure that you have not lost your place and that you are marking in the row numbered the same as the question you are answering.

6) Read the questions

Be sure you know what the question asks! Many capable people are unsuccessful because they failed to *read* the questions correctly.

7) Answer all questions

Unless you have been instructed that a penalty will be deducted for incorrect answers, it is better to guess than to omit a question.

8) Speed tests

It is often better NOT to guess on speed tests. It has been found that on timed tests people are tempted to spend the last few seconds before time is called in marking answers at random – without even reading them – in the hope of picking up a few extra points. To discourage this practice, the instructions may warn you that your score will be "corrected" for guessing. That is, a penalty will be applied. The incorrect answers will be deducted from the correct ones, or some other penalty formula will be used.

9) Review your answers

If you finish before time is called, go back to the questions you guessed or omitted to give them further thought. Review other answers if you have time.

10) Return your test materials

If you are ready to leave before others have finished or time is called, take ALL your materials to the monitor and leave quietly. Never take any test material with you. The monitor can discover whose papers are not complete, and taking a test booklet may be grounds for disqualification.

VIII. EXAMINATION TECHNIQUES

1) Read the general instructions carefully. These are usually printed on the first page of the exam booklet. As a rule, these instructions refer to the timing of the examination; the fact that you should not start work until the signal and must stop work at a signal, etc. If there are any *special* instructions, such as a choice of questions to be answered, make sure that you note this instruction carefully.

2) When you are ready to start work on the examination, that is as soon as the signal has been given, read the instructions to each question booklet, underline any key words or phrases, such as *least*, *best*, *outline*, *describe* and the like. In this way you will tend to answer as requested rather than discover on reviewing your paper that you *listed without describing*, that you selected the *worst* choice rather than the *best* choice, etc.

3) If the examination is of the objective or multiple-choice type – that is, each question will also give a series of possible answers: A, B, C or D, and you are called upon to select the best answer and write the letter next to that answer on your answer paper – it is advisable to start answering each question in turn. There may be anywhere from 50 to 100 such questions in the three or four hours allotted and you can see how much time would be taken if you read through all the questions before beginning to answer any. Furthermore, if you come across a question or group of questions which you know would be difficult to answer, it would undoubtedly affect your handling of all the other questions.

4) If the examination is of the essay type and contains but a few questions, it is a moot point as to whether you should read all the questions before starting to answer any one. Of course, if you are given a choice – say five out of seven and the like – then it is essential to read all the questions so you can eliminate the two that are most difficult. If, however, you are asked to answer all the questions, there may be danger in trying to answer the easiest one first because you may find that you will spend too much time on it. The best technique is to answer the first question, then proceed to the second, etc.

5) Time your answers. Before the exam begins, write down the time it started, then add the time allowed for the examination and write down the time it must be completed, then divide the time available somewhat as follows:

- If 3-1/2 hours are allowed, that would be 210 minutes. If you have 80 objective-type questions, that would be an average of 2-1/2 minutes per question. Allow yourself no more than 2 minutes per question, or a total of 160 minutes, which will permit about 50 minutes to review.
- If for the time allotment of 210 minutes there are 7 essay questions to answer, that would average about 30 minutes a question. Give yourself only 25 minutes per question so that you have about 35 minutes to review.

6) The most important instruction is to *read each question* and make sure you know what is wanted. The second most important instruction is to *time yourself properly* so that you answer every question. The third most important instruction is to *answer every question*. Guess if you have to but include something for each question. Remember that you will receive no credit for a blank and will probably receive some credit if you write something in answer to an essay question. If you guess a letter – say "B" for a multiple-choice question – you may have guessed right. If you leave a blank as an answer to a multiple-choice question, the examiners may respect your feelings but it will not add a point to your score. Some exams may penalize you for wrong answers, so in such cases *only*, you may not want to guess unless you have some basis for your answer.

7) Suggestions
   a. Objective-type questions
      1. Examine the question booklet for proper sequence of pages and questions
      2. Read all instructions carefully
      3. Skip any question which seems too difficult; return to it after all other questions have been answered
      4. Apportion your time properly; do not spend too much time on any single question or group of questions
      5. Note and underline key words – *all, most, fewest, least, best, worst, same, opposite,* etc.
      6. Pay particular attention to negatives
      7. Note unusual option, e.g., unduly long, short, complex, different or similar in content to the body of the question
      8. Observe the use of "hedging" words – *probably, may, most likely,* etc.
      9. Make sure that your answer is put next to the same number as the question
      10. Do not second-guess unless you have good reason to believe the second answer is definitely more correct
      11. Cross out original answer if you decide another answer is more accurate; do not erase until you are ready to hand your paper in
      12. Answer all questions; guess unless instructed otherwise
      13. Leave time for review

   b. Essay questions
      1. Read each question carefully
      2. Determine exactly what is wanted. Underline key words or phrases.
      3. Decide on outline or paragraph answer

4. Include many different points and elements unless asked to develop any one or two points or elements
5. Show impartiality by giving pros and cons unless directed to select one side only
6. Make and write down any assumptions you find necessary to answer the questions
7. Watch your English, grammar, punctuation and choice of words
8. Time your answers; don't crowd material

8) Answering the essay question

Most essay questions can be answered by framing the specific response around several key words or ideas. Here are a few such key words or ideas:

M's: manpower, materials, methods, money, management
P's: purpose, program, policy, plan, procedure, practice, problems, pitfalls, personnel, public relations

  a. Six basic steps in handling problems:
    1. Preliminary plan and background development
    2. Collect information, data and facts
    3. Analyze and interpret information, data and facts
    4. Analyze and develop solutions as well as make recommendations
    5. Prepare report and sell recommendations
    6. Install recommendations and follow up effectiveness

  b. Pitfalls to avoid
    1. *Taking things for granted* – A statement of the situation does not necessarily imply that each of the elements is necessarily true; for example, a complaint may be invalid and biased so that all that can be taken for granted is that a complaint has been registered
    2. *Considering only one side of a situation* – Wherever possible, indicate several alternatives and then point out the reasons you selected the best one
    3. *Failing to indicate follow up* – Whenever your answer indicates action on your part, make certain that you will take proper follow-up action to see how successful your recommendations, procedures or actions turn out to be
    4. *Taking too long in answering any single question* – Remember to time your answers properly

IX. AFTER THE TEST

Scoring procedures differ in detail among civil service jurisdictions although the general principles are the same. Whether the papers are hand-scored or graded by machine we have described, they are nearly always graded by number. That is, the person who marks the paper knows only the number – never the name – of the applicant. Not until all the papers have been graded will they be matched with names. If other tests, such as training and experience or oral interview ratings have been given, scores will be combined. Different parts of the examination usually have different weights. For example, the written test might count 60 percent of the final grade, and a rating of training and experience 40 percent. In many jurisdictions, veterans will have a certain number of points added to their grades.

After the final grade has been determined, the names are placed in grade order and an eligible list is established. There are various methods for resolving ties between those who get the same final grade – probably the most common is to place first the name of the person whose application was received first. Job offers are made from the eligible list in the order the names appear on it. You will be notified of your grade and your rank as soon as all these computations have been made. This will be done as rapidly as possible.

People who are found to meet the requirements in the announcement are called "eligibles." Their names are put on a list of eligible candidates. An eligible's chances of getting a job depend on how high he stands on this list and how fast agencies are filling jobs from the list.

When a job is to be filled from a list of eligibles, the agency asks for the names of people on the list of eligibles for that job. When the civil service commission receives this request, it sends to the agency the names of the three people highest on this list. Or, if the job to be filled has specialized requirements, the office sends the agency the names of the top three persons who meet these requirements from the general list.

The appointing officer makes a choice from among the three people whose names were sent to him. If the selected person accepts the appointment, the names of the others are put back on the list to be considered for future openings.

That is the rule in hiring from all kinds of eligible lists, whether they are for typist, carpenter, chemist, or something else. For every vacancy, the appointing officer has his choice of any one of the top three eligibles on the list. This explains why the person whose name is on top of the list sometimes does not get an appointment when some of the persons lower on the list do. If the appointing officer chooses the second or third eligible, the No. 1 eligible does not get a job at once, but stays on the list until he is appointed or the list is terminated.

X. HOW TO PASS THE INTERVIEW TEST

The examination for which you applied requires an oral interview test. You have already taken the written test and you are now being called for the interview test – the final part of the formal examination.

You may think that it is not possible to prepare for an interview test and that there are no procedures to follow during an interview. Our purpose is to point out some things you can do in advance that will help you and some good rules to follow and pitfalls to avoid while you are being interviewed.

What is an interview supposed to test?

The written examination is designed to test the technical knowledge and competence of the candidate; the oral is designed to evaluate intangible qualities, not readily measured otherwise, and to establish a list showing the relative fitness of each candidate – as measured against his competitors – for the position sought. Scoring is not on the basis of "right" and "wrong," but on a sliding scale of values ranging from "not passable" to "outstanding." As a matter of fact, it is possible to achieve a relatively low score without a single "incorrect" answer because of evident weakness in the qualities being measured.

Occasionally, an examination may consist entirely of an oral test – either an individual or a group oral. In such cases, information is sought concerning the technical knowledges and abilities of the candidate, since there has been no written examination for this purpose. More commonly, however, an oral test is used to supplement a written examination.

Who conducts interviews?

The composition of oral boards varies among different jurisdictions. In nearly all, a representative of the personnel department serves as chairman. One of the members of the board may be a representative of the department in which the candidate would work. In some cases, "outside experts" are used, and, frequently, a businessman or some other representative of the general public is asked to serve. Labor and management or other special groups may be represented. The aim is to secure the services of experts in the appropriate field.

However the board is composed, it is a good idea (and not at all improper or unethical) to ascertain in advance of the interview who the members are and what groups they represent. When you are introduced to them, you will have some idea of their backgrounds and interests, and at least you will not stutter and stammer over their names.

What should be done before the interview?

While knowledge about the board members is useful and takes some of the surprise element out of the interview, there is other preparation which is more substantive. It *is* possible to prepare for an oral interview – in several ways:

1) Keep a copy of your application and review it carefully before the interview

This may be the only document before the oral board, and the starting point of the interview. Know what education and experience you have listed there, and the sequence and dates of all of it. Sometimes the board will ask you to review the highlights of your experience for them; you should not have to hem and haw doing it.

2) Study the class specification and the examination announcement

Usually, the oral board has one or both of these to guide them. The qualities, characteristics or knowledges required by the position sought are stated in these documents. They offer valuable clues as to the nature of the oral interview. For example, if the job involves supervisory responsibilities, the announcement will usually indicate that knowledge of modern supervisory methods and the qualifications of the candidate as a supervisor will be tested. If so, you can expect such questions, frequently in the form of a hypothetical situation which you are expected to solve. NEVER go into an oral without knowledge of the duties and responsibilities of the job you seek.

3) Think through each qualification required

Try to visualize the kind of questions you would ask if you were a board member. How well could you answer them? Try especially to appraise your own knowledge and background in each area, *measured against the job sought*, and identify any areas in which you are weak. Be critical and realistic – do not flatter yourself.

4) Do some general reading in areas in which you feel you may be weak

For example, if the job involves supervision and your past experience has NOT, some general reading in supervisory methods and practices, particularly in the field of human relations, might be useful. Do NOT study agency procedures or detailed manuals. The oral board will be testing your understanding and capacity, not your memory.

5) Get a good night's sleep and watch your general health and mental attitude

You will want a clear head at the interview. Take care of a cold or any other minor ailment, and of course, no hangovers.

What should be done on the day of the interview?

Now comes the day of the interview itself. Give yourself plenty of time to get there. Plan to arrive somewhat ahead of the scheduled time, particularly if your appointment is in the fore part of the day. If a previous candidate fails to appear, the board might be ready for you a bit early. By early afternoon an oral board is almost invariably behind schedule if there are many candidates, and you may have to wait. Take along a book or magazine to read, or your application to review, but leave any extraneous material in the waiting room when you go in for your interview. In any event, relax and compose yourself.

The matter of dress is important. The board is forming impressions about you – from your experience, your manners, your attitude, and your appearance. Give your personal appearance careful attention. Dress your best, but not your flashiest. Choose conservative, appropriate clothing, and be sure it is immaculate. This is a business interview, and your appearance should indicate that you regard it as such. Besides, being well groomed and properly dressed will help boost your confidence.

Sooner or later, someone will call your name and escort you into the interview room. *This is it.* From here on you are on your own. It is too late for any more preparation. But remember, you asked for this opportunity to prove your fitness, and you are here because your request was granted.

What happens when you go in?

The usual sequence of events will be as follows: The clerk (who is often the board stenographer) will introduce you to the chairman of the oral board, who will introduce you to the other members of the board. Acknowledge the introductions before you sit down. Do not be surprised if you find a microphone facing you or a stenotypist sitting by. Oral interviews are usually recorded in the event of an appeal or other review.

Usually the chairman of the board will open the interview by reviewing the highlights of your education and work experience from your application – primarily for the benefit of the other members of the board, as well as to get the material into the record. Do not interrupt or comment unless there is an error or significant misinterpretation; if that is the case, do not hesitate. But do not quibble about insignificant matters. Also, he will usually ask you some question about your education, experience or your present job – partly to get you to start talking and to establish the interviewing "rapport." He may start the actual questioning, or turn it over to one of the other members. Frequently, each member undertakes the questioning on a particular area, one in which he is perhaps most competent, so you can expect each member to participate in the examination. Because time is limited, you may also expect some rather abrupt switches in the direction the questioning takes, so do not be upset by it. Normally, a board member will not pursue a single line of questioning unless he discovers a particular strength or weakness.

After each member has participated, the chairman will usually ask whether any member has any further questions, then will ask you if you have anything you wish to add. Unless you are expecting this question, it may floor you. Worse, it may start you off on an extended, extemporaneous speech. The board is not usually seeking more information. The question is principally to offer you a last opportunity to present further qualifications or to indicate that you have nothing to add. So, if you feel that a significant qualification or characteristic has been overlooked, it is proper to point it out in a sentence or so. Do not compliment the board on the thoroughness of their examination – they have been sketchy, and you know it. If you wish, merely say, "No thank you, I have nothing further to add." This is a point where you can "talk yourself out" of a good impression or fail to present an important bit of information. Remember, *you close the interview yourself.*

The chairman will then say, "That is all, Mr. _____, thank you." Do not be startled; the interview is over, and quicker than you think. Thank him, gather your belongings and take your leave. Save your sigh of relief for the other side of the door.

How to put your best foot forward

Throughout this entire process, you may feel that the board individually and collectively is trying to pierce your defenses, seek out your hidden weaknesses and embarrass and confuse you. Actually, this is not true. They are obliged to make an appraisal of your qualifications for the job you are seeking, and they want to see you in your best light. Remember, they must interview all candidates and a non-cooperative candidate may become a failure in spite of their best efforts to bring out his qualifications. Here are 15 suggestions that will help you:

1) Be natural – Keep your attitude confident, not cocky

If you are not confident that you can do the job, do not expect the board to be. Do not apologize for your weaknesses, try to bring out your strong points. The board is interested in a positive, not negative, presentation. Cockiness will antagonize any board member and make him wonder if you are covering up a weakness by a false show of strength.

2) Get comfortable, but don't lounge or sprawl

Sit erectly but not stiffly. A careless posture may lead the board to conclude that you are careless in other things, or at least that you are not impressed by the importance of the occasion. Either conclusion is natural, even if incorrect. Do not fuss with your clothing, a pencil or an ashtray. Your hands may occasionally be useful to emphasize a point; do not let them become a point of distraction.

3) Do not wisecrack or make small talk

This is a serious situation, and your attitude should show that you consider it as such. Further, the time of the board is limited – they do not want to waste it, and neither should you.

4) Do not exaggerate your experience or abilities

In the first place, from information in the application or other interviews and sources, the board may know more about you than you think. Secondly, you probably will not get away with it. An experienced board is rather adept at spotting such a situation, so do not take the chance.

5) If you know a board member, do not make a point of it, yet do not hide it

Certainly you are not fooling him, and probably not the other members of the board. Do not try to take advantage of your acquaintanceship – it will probably do you little good.

6) Do not dominate the interview

Let the board do that. They will give you the clues – do not assume that you have to do all the talking. Realize that the board has a number of questions to ask you, and do not try to take up all the interview time by showing off your extensive knowledge of the answer to the first one.

7) Be attentive

You only have 20 minutes or so, and you should keep your attention at its sharpest throughout. When a member is addressing a problem or question to you, give him your undivided attention. Address your reply principally to him, but do not exclude the other board members.

8) Do not interrupt

A board member may be stating a problem for you to analyze. He will ask you a question when the time comes. Let him state the problem, and wait for the question.

9) Make sure you understand the question

Do not try to answer until you are sure what the question is. If it is not clear, restate it in your own words or ask the board member to clarify it for you. However, do not haggle about minor elements.

10) Reply promptly but not hastily

A common entry on oral board rating sheets is "candidate responded readily," or "candidate hesitated in replies." Respond as promptly and quickly as you can, but do not jump to a hasty, ill-considered answer.

11) Do not be peremptory in your answers

A brief answer is proper – but do not fire your answer back. That is a losing game from your point of view. The board member can probably ask questions much faster than you can answer them.

12) Do not try to create the answer you think the board member wants

He is interested in what kind of mind you have and how it works – not in playing games. Furthermore, he can usually spot this practice and will actually grade you down on it.

13) Do not switch sides in your reply merely to agree with a board member

Frequently, a member will take a contrary position merely to draw you out and to see if you are willing and able to defend your point of view. Do not start a debate, yet do not surrender a good position. If a position is worth taking, it is worth defending.

14) Do not be afraid to admit an error in judgment if you are shown to be wrong

The board knows that you are forced to reply without any opportunity for careful consideration. Your answer may be demonstrably wrong. If so, admit it and get on with the interview.

15) Do not dwell at length on your present job

The opening question may relate to your present assignment. Answer the question but do not go into an extended discussion. You are being examined for a *new* job, not your present one. As a matter of fact, try to phrase ALL your answers in terms of the job for which you are being examined.

Basis of Rating

Probably you will forget most of these "do's" and "don'ts" when you walk into the oral interview room. Even remembering them all will not ensure you a passing grade. Perhaps you did not have the qualifications in the first place. But remembering them will help you to put your best foot forward, without treading on the toes of the board members.

Rumor and popular opinion to the contrary notwithstanding, an oral board wants you to make the best appearance possible. They know you are under pressure – but they also want to see how you respond to it as a guide to what your reaction would be under the pressures of the job you seek. They will be influenced by the degree of poise you display, the personal traits you show and the manner in which you respond.

ABOUT THIS BOOK

This book contains tests divided into Examination Sections. Go through each test, answering every question in the margin. At the end of each test look at the answer key and check your answers. On the ones you got wrong, look at the right answer choice and learn. Do not fill in the answers first. Do not memorize the questions and answers, but understand the answer and principles involved. On your test, the questions will likely be different from the samples. Questions are changed and new ones added. If you understand these past questions you should have success with any changes that arise. Tests may consist of several types of questions. We have additional books on each subject should more study be advisable or necessary for you. Finally, the more you study, the better prepared you will be. This book is intended to be the last thing you study before you walk into the examination room. Prior study of relevant texts is also recommended. NLC publishes some of these in our Fundamental Series. Knowledge and good sense are important factors in passing your exam. Good luck also helps. So now study this Passbook, absorb the material contained within and take that knowledge into the examination. Then do your best to pass that exam.

EXAMINATION SECTION

EXAMINATION SECTION
TEST 1

DIRECTIONS: Each question or incomplete statement is followed by several suggested answers or completions. Select the one that BEST answers the question or completes the statement. *PRINT THE LETTER OF THE CORRECT ANSWER IN THE SPACE AT THE RIGHT.*

1. The frontage of old law tenements GENERALLY is _____ feet.

    A. over 100
    B. between 50 feet and 100
    C. between 35 feet and 50
    D. less than 35

2. A cellar is that portion of a building which

    A. is 100% below curb level
    B. must have more than half of its height below curb level
    C. may be at grade with the curb level, but is the lowest floor in a building
    D. must have at least half of its height above curb level

3. An owner who refuses to permit an assessor entry to his building during a reasonable hour of vistitation may face a penalty of

    A. imprisonment of up to six months
    B. a fine of up to $5,000
    C. imprisonment of not more than 30 days and/or a fine of not more than $50
    D. imprisonment of up to six months and/or a fine of up to $500

4. Assume that a lease for 10 years at $10,000 per year is to be sold at a price to yield 10% to the purchaser.
    The following factors are known:
    I. The future worth of $1 is .25937
    II. The future worth of $1 per annum is 15.9374
    III. The present worth of $1 is .3855
    IV. The present worth of $1 per annum is 6.145
    The value of the aforementioned lease is

    A. $25,937   B. $38,550   C. $61,450   D. $159,374

5. No later than the twenty-fifth day of each June, the real property tax rate is fixed to raise the amount not provided by general fund revenue receipts in order to meet city budget requirements.
    This tax rate is fixed by the

    A. comptroller
    B. tax commission
    C. city clerk
    D. city council

6. Pursuant to the real property tax law, the legal bases for reviewing an assessment in the state are illegality, overvaluation, and inequality.
    For a property owner to establish a case of overvaluation, he MUST prove that the

A. assessed valuation contested is greater than the full value of the property
B. relationship between the assessed valuation contested and the full value of the property is greater than the relationship between the assessed valuation and the full value for similar properties in the taxing district
C. assessed valuation contested produces a real estate tax that is too great a burden to maintain the property
D. subject property, in relation to its market value, bears the highest tax burden on the block

7. A property has a land assessment of $100,000 and a total assessment of $150,000. In contesting this assessment, the one of the following allegations which, if proven by the owner, would have the MOST relevance to his case would be that the

   A. market value of the land is $100,000 and is the entire value of this property
   B. market value of the land alone is $75,000
   C. improvements on the land have a current full value of $30,000
   D. land was purchased five years ago for $60,000 and it cost $75,000 to construct the buildings located on the land

8. Owners of residential buildings occupied by three or more families for permanent residence purposes may obtain tax benefits when making certain building alterations or improvements.
   Which one of the following would NOT entitle the owner to this tax benefit?

   A. Painting the building
   B. Replacing the plumbing in the building
   C. Installation of a new heating system
   D. Replacing the elevator lines in the building

9. In the field of real estate taxation, *price* and *value* have different connotations. Select the one of the following statements which BEST expresses the difference in meaning of these two terms as they relate to real estate taxation. Price is _____; value is _____.

   A. what the buyer pays for the property; the amount the seller believes the property is worth
   B. determined by short-term factors and by caprices of the market; dependent on long-term factors and resists the impact of temporary and abnormal conditions
   C. the amount the buyer pays under ordinary circumstances; the amount for which the property would sell under the most favorable circumstances
   D. the amount agreed upon by the buyer and seller in a market place transaction; the estimate of worth determined by competent appraisers

10. The equalization rate represents the relationships of assessments to full value in a particular assessing district.
    Which one of the following statements is CORRECT in reference to equalization in the city?

    A. Property owners who are challenging the tax commission's application of equalization to their property are not entitled to know whether the tax commission has fixed equalization rates, pursuant to the Administrative Code.

B. The tax commission must fix equalization rates for the valuation of property so as to establish a just and equal relation throughout the entire city and need not consider borough differences.
C. The tax commissioner in each borough must accept the equalization rate established by the state as the measure of relationship of assessment to full value in his borough.
D. Property owners contesting equalization of assessment of their property are not entitled to inquire into the methods and procedures employed by assessors in arriving at the assessment challenged.

11. In some situations, personalty annexed to the structure becomes part of the real estate and is subject to real property taxation.
Which one of the following is personalty which should be assessed as real property?

    A. Office building tenants' installation of interior partitions, additional electrical wiring, and acoustical ceilings
    B. Wall mirrors on wood frames in a beauty salon
    C. A bank vault installed by a lessee bank and where real property taxes are paid by the lessor
    D. Seats in a theater or exhibition hall

12. Applications for correction of assessed valuations are the taxpayer's method of formally requesting a review of his assessment.
Which one of the following is CORRECT with regard to the application process?

    A. The assessor sends properly completed applications for correction of assessed valuation directly to the tax commission for the scheduling of hearings.
    B. Applications for correction of assessed valuations must be made under oath, on forms furnished by the real property assessment department.
    C. The city has two forms of applications. One form is to be submitted for all residential property and vacant land. The other is to be submitted for all commercial (non-residential), industrial, and utility properties.
    D. If a hearing before the tax commission is desired, a separate letter requesting this must accompany the application.

13. Errors in assessments or taxes on real property may be due to a clerical mistake or an error of description contained in the several books of annual record of assessed valuations, or in the assessment rolls.
Such errors may be corrected by the

    A. assessor-in-charge, since he has the responsibility of examining all field books of assessors
    B. tax commission, which is charged with the duty of reviewing and correcting all assessments of real property for taxation
    C. finance administrator, to whom the Administrative Code also grants authorization to refund or credit the difference between the taxes computed on the erroneous and corrected assessments
    D. comptroller, to whom the president of the city council has given notification of the amount of taxes in each book of assessment rolls

14. An assessor has made a complete market study of a particular neighborhood in his district and believes that assessed valuations should be increased considerably over the past year because the market value has risen.
The assessor, prior to reporting and entering his increased valuations, is REQUIRED to

    A. prepare an affidavit attesting to the results of his market study for submission to the finance administration
    B. check to see if price level indices for similar neighborhoods in other districts have experienced the same percentage of increase and report the statistics to the tax commission
    C. show all comparable sales applicable to each property in the field book
    D. advise the technical assistant who must consult with the assessor-in-charge

15. According to the Administrative Code, the individual who is charged GENERALLY with the duty and responsibility of assessing all real property subject to taxation within the city is the

    A. finance administrator
    B. president of the tax commission
    C. director of the city record
    D. president of the city council

16. The City Charter provides for the review and correction of assessments of real property for taxation.
To which of the following does the Charter assign this duty?
The

    A. tax commission
    B. finance administrator
    C. board of estimate
    D. comptroller

17. Assessors, in establishing assessed valuations must thoroughly analyze and consider construction costs. The unit cost for various types of structures should be

    A. developed from the assessor's interviews with builders and contractors in his district
    B. obtained from the technical assistant to whom they are furnished by the research bureau
    C. compiled from the assessor's own study of various building cost services on file in the real property assessment department office
    D. derived from actual new construction cost data on record in the building department for those structures that have been built in the assessor's district

18. According to the Administrative Code, each assessor provides a statement to the finance administrator as to the sum for which, in his judgment, each separately assessed parcel of real estate would sell.
According to the Code, the assessor must consider each sale

    A. as it is influenced by prevailing market conditions as of the twenty-fifth day of January in each year
    B. taking into account the price levels of similar real estate as of the date of tax roll certification on the twentieth day of June of the previous tax year

C. as occurring under ordinary circumstances, if the parcel were wholly unimproved, or with the improvements, if any, thereon
D. with reference to the *willing buyer/willing seller* concept when neither economic depression nor boom is manifested

19. The landlord's information return, filed with the finance administration, is a(n) 19._____

    A. itemized listing of the rentals for all units in an apartment house
    B. report by the landlord as to major capital improvements he has made to the building he owns
    C. notice that the owner intends to convert an apartment building into a condominium prior to February 1
    D. valuable source of rental data for commercial properties

20. An owner of vacant land has received an exemption because he has previously expressed an intention to build upon or develop it. 20._____
    An assessor must examine the property and

    A. advise the owner that if construction is not started by January 25, the tax commission will restore the property to the tax roll
    B. if he finds that construction has not been started, submit a query sheet for each year that the property remains unimproved
    C. obtain from the owner a new application every two years during the protest period if construction has not started
    D. advise the technical assistant who shall consult the research bureau as to whether current zoning will still permit intended construction

21. If property is exempt from real estate taxation pursuant to the real property tax law, but if any portion of the property is not used exclusively to carry out one or more of its exempt purposes, but is leased or otherwise used for other purposes, such portion shall be subject to taxation and the remaining portion only shall be exempt. However, there are exceptions to the above rule. 21._____
    The one of the following situations which is NOT a valid exception to the rule is when a(n)

    A. exempt institution leases space to the United Nations
    B. exempt institution leases part of its land to a *not-for-profit* housing company
    C. free public hospital depending on charity for its support leases space in the hospital for purposes of income but uses this income to help support and maintain the hospital
    D. exempt religious institution leases part of its property to a private day camp whose rental payments are used for the support and maintenance of the religious institution

22. A new category of exemption has been established for multiple dwellings constructed in the city if these properties meet certain eligibility requirements. 22._____
    The one of the following statements relating to eligibility which is INCORRECT is that

    A. to establish eligibility there is a time limit as to the construction and completion dates
    B. multi-family dwellings of seven or more units are eligible

C. the city housing and development administration must certify as to the eligibility
D. rentals to be charged in the new facility shall be 15 percent or less than those of comparable facilities

23. No assessor shall, of his own accord, exempt a parcel of real estate which has heretofore been taxable.
The power to grant exemption is vested ONLY in the

A. tax commission
B. finance administrator
C. city council
D. assessor-in-charge of the borough

24. The LAST date on which a property owner can file an application for correction of assessed valuation is

A. March 15
B. April 15
C. June 30
D. October 30

25. A two-story office building is being constructed in the city, but has not been completed on January 25, 2018. Under which one of the following conditions could this property be assessed for real estate taxes for the ensuing year?

A. The building will be ready for occupancy on May 1, 2018.
B. All space in the building has already been leased to tenants whose occupancy may begin on May 1, 2018, when the building will be completed.
C. The building will be ready for occupancy on April 15, 2018 but only 10% of the space will be occupied on that date.
D. One tenant has leased all the space in the building in a contract signed on April 15, 2018, and has paid three months rent as security but occupancy does not begin until some time in the future.

26. In order to complete the assessment roll and at the same time provide a reasonable period for property owners to check their assessments, file applications for correction, have hearings and if necessary initiate court actions, certain dates have been established for orderly procedures. Which one of the following does NOT represent an accurate date in these procedures?

A. January 25 is taxable status day.
B. Assessment rolls are available for inspection from February 1 through March 15.
C. Final assessed valuations are open for inspection on May 25.
D. Petitions for review of tax assessments on real property must be served on the tax commission on or before June 30.

27. In the cost approach, the building value is computed by

A. deducting the land value from the purchase price
B. estimating the original construction cost of the building and deducting the depreciation
C. estimating the present construction cost less depreciation
D. computing the land to building ratio which is prevalent in the area

28. The economic rent is the

   A. least possible rental a prospective tenant can negotiate
   B. rental expressed in the lease, and based on a percentage of the sales or business done in the premises
   C. fair market rental for the leased premises
   D. highest rent indicated by the *cost of living index*

29. In valuing an apartment building by comparing it to similar apartment buildings, an indication of the loss of building value due to economic obsolescence is reflected by the differences in

   A. physical conditions of the units
   B. replacement cost less depreciation
   C. operating costs per unit
   D. rentals per unit

30. The value of a leasehold is the

   A. present worth of the economic rent, less the contract rent, for the unexpired term of the lease
   B. total difference between the rental reserved in the lease and a market value rental for the premises
   C. present worth of the rentals reserved in the lease
   D. value of the reversion at the expiration of the lease

31. Capitalization is BEST defined as

   A. the acquisition of funds to finance a purchase
   B. the financial strength of the property owner
   C. the conversion of anticipated net income into present value
   D. working capital

32. The following are data concerning four buildings:

   I. Building #1, new, will cost $13,000,000
      Gross rentals will produce an estimated 3,000,000
      Income attributable to land 400,000
   II. Building #2, new, will cost $13,300,000
      Gross rentals will produce an estimated 3,100,000
      Income attributable to land 380,000
   III. Building #3, new, will cost $16,000,000
      Gross rentals will produce an estimated 3,700,000
      Income attributable to land 360,000
   IV. Building #4, new, will cost $15,000,000
      Gross rentals will produce an estimated 3,300,000
      Income attributable to land 300,000

   Based upon the data presented above, which building would represent the HIGHEST and BEST use of the land? Building

   A. #1   B. #2   C. #3   D. #4

33. An analysis of three similar properties produces the following data:

Sale #	Net Income	Sale Price
1	$36,000	$300,000
2	$39,100	$340,000
3	$60,000	$500,000

    The above data permit the derivation of a(n)

    A. gross rental multiple
    B. overall capitalization rate
    C. economic rental value
    D. operating ratio

34. The BEST sales trend indicators for any given geographical area are

    A. local cost indices
    B. comparisons of subject properties with sales of similar properties
    C. sales and resales of subject properties
    D. published data relating to institutional mortgages

35. For retail store properties, the BEST unit for analysis of comparable sales is generally

    A. cubic foot value
    B. volume of business done
    C. unit lot value
    D. value per front foot

36. A deed has affixed $33 of state document tax stamps and recites: Subject to an existing mortgage of $40,000, and a purchase money, subordinate mortgage of $20,000 delivered this date as part of the consideration.
    The actual cash paid was

    A. $10,000   B. $30,000   C. $60,000   D. $70,000

37. The term *vacuum return system* refers to a type of _____ system.

    A. heating
    B. sprinkler
    C. cable TV
    D. electrical wiring

38. The term *floor area ratio* can BEST be defined as the ratio of the

    A. number of permitted floors in a building to the size of the zoning lot
    B. area of a typical floor to the height of a typical floor
    C. total permitted building area on a zoning lot to the area of that zoning lot
    D. street frontage of a zoning lot to the area of that zoning lot

39. When training subordinates who show high work potential, it is sometimes a good idea to assign them a bit more work than they can handle.
    This technique is GENERALLY useful because it

    A. will identify those subordinates who cannot keep up with the department's work load
    B. is a good incentive for self-discovery and self-development
    C. will teach subordinates to be less concerned about mistakes than they have been
    D. is a means of strengthening a subordinate's weak points

40. In order to provide effective on-the-job training for his subordinates, the FIRST step an assessor should take is to   40._____

    A. present the job to his subordinates one step at a time
    B. select the materials to be used in the training program
    C. make a complete and detailed breakdown of the job to be taught
    D. set up a timetable of instructions and follow it

KEY (CORRECT ANSWERS)

1. D	11. C	21. D	31. C
2. B	12. B	22. B	32. A
3. C	13. C	23. A	33. B
4. C	14. D	24. A	34. C
5. D	15. A	25. C	35. D
6. A	16. A	26. D	36. A
7. A	17. B	27. C	37. A
8. A	18. C	28. C	38. C
9. B	19. D	29. D	39. B
10. D	20. B	30. A	40. C

EXAMINATION SECTION
TEST 1

DIRECTIONS: Each question or incomplete statement is followed by several suggested answers or completions. Select the one that BEST answers the question or completes the statement. *PRINT THE LETTER OF THE CORRECT ANSWER IN THE SPACE AT THE RIGHT.*

1. In the assessment of a single-family attached home, seven sales of similar property at the following prices are noted: $231,000, $234,000, $232,000, $232,500, $228,700, $230,500, and $228,000.
   The MEDIAN sales price of these properties is

   A. $231,500   B. $230,750   C. $239,951   D. $231,000

2. A study of sales trends in a neighborhood indicates the following data on average prices (2010 - base year):

Year	Price Index
2010	1.00
2011	1.10
2012	1.32
2013	1.20
2014	1.15

   All other things being equal, if a parcel sold for $100,000 in 2011, it would have an EQUIVALENT price in 2014 of
   A. $115,000   B. $104,545   C. $104,498   D. $101,500

3. For an object to have value in an economic sense, it must

   A. be visually attractive
   B. have utility and relative scarcity
   C. have a clear title
   D. be scarce and be transferrable

4. The *principle of change* is evidenced in the

   A. use of one interest rate for mortgage and a different one for equity
   B. building residual technique
   C. various forms of land ownership
   D. evolutionary stages in the life of a neighborhood

5. In determining whether property is personal rather than real, the one of the following factors which is NOT pertinent is the

   A. relative cost of the property as compared to value of land on which it is located
   B. use and occupancy of the premises
   C. manner in which the property is attached to the land
   D. intention of the party who installed the property in the premises

6. The one of the following statements about the *principle of substitution* which is MOST accurate is that it   6.____

   A. has application to the three approaches to value
   B. is no longer accepted by the courts
   C. affirms that when a builder cannot get specified material, he may substitute other material reasonably similar
   D. relates to the alternate choices in capitalization rate selection

7. The one of the following statements which is MOST valid about the *principle of anticipation* in its application to the appraisal of real property is that it   7.____

   A. affirms that change is ever present, especially with regard to rental projections
   B. states that excess profits breed ruinous competition
   C. affirms that value is the present worth of future benefits
   D. provides the basis for the use of escalator clauses in leases

8. Sales assessment ratios, compiled from a statistical analysis of sales data, are LEAST likely to reveal the validity of the   8.____

   A. level or levels of assessed valuations
   B. equality of assessments in various areas of the assessing district
   C. sales data itself to sale/purchase motivations
   D. cost and depreciation factors used in assessing property

9. The *purpose* of an appraisal should be included as a section in the final report CHIEFLY to   9.____

   A. give a short summary of the approach used to determine value
   B. provide the basis for fixing the appraiser's compensation
   C. indicate the destination of the report
   D. set forth the reason for making the appraisal

10. The income capitalization evaluation approach is MOST valid when applied to a   10.____

    A. taxpayer   B. townhouse
    C. two-family dwelling   D. condominium unit

11. Which of the following is the BEST source of demographic data?   11.____

    A. Chamber of Commerce reports
    B. F.H.A. Rental Surveys
    C. U.S. Census Tract Studies
    D. Real Estate Board Tracts

12. In general, the one of the following statements about rental conditions in city neighborhoods which is MOST valid is that they   12.____

    A. follow national trends
    B. may indicate trends which do not necessarily correspond to regional and national trends
    C. may lag behind national trends but will eventually coincide with them
    D. do not always follow national trends but follow regional trends

13. *Highest and best use* of land can be defined as the   13.____

    A. most intensive use under urban renewal plans
    B. use which produces the largest gross income
    C. use which permits the largest building compatible with zoning provisions
    D. most profitable use

14. The *Bundle of Rights* relates to   14.____

    A. rights of tenants under rent laws
    B. constitutional authority to appropriate real property
    C. various rights attached to ownership of real estate
    D. four rights which state governments possess with regard to real estate

15. *Plottage* is GENERALLY considered an incremental influence in the appraisal of   15.____

    A. a 40-by-100-foot parcel in a single-family home area
    B. a 30-foot corner parcel at the intersection of two major retail streets
    C. two or more contiguous lots held under single ownership and utility
    D. a corner lot with a depth of 118 feet

16. If an independent appraiser in need of sales information does not have access to the published sales data, he can BEST obtain the information he needs by   16.____

    A. securing sales data from assessors' cards in the finance administration
    B. consulting sales data in the county clerk's register's office
    C. reviewing the newspaper accounts of sales
    D. examining the city sales tax records

17. *Appraisal area,* as used in local courts, might BEST be defined as the actual area   17.____

    A. computed by the appraiser
    B. adjusted for various increments and depth factors
    C. adjusted for locational amenities
    D. stipulated by both sides in litigation

18. The term *trending* means adjusting sales data for the   18.____

    A. time of sale
    B. physical characteristics of the building
    C. locational factors involved
    D. shape and depth of the lot

19. When sales data is exchanged prior to a trial on assessment appeal, it MUST include   19.____

    A. name of the grantor's attorney
    B. date sale was confirmed
    C. appraiser's rating of *comparable* as compared to *subject*
    D. date and page of recorded instrument

20. Confirmation of sales information as evidence of value is accomplished when   20.____

    A. a copy of the closing statement is obtained
    B. title actually passes

C. ownership changes appear on the assessment roll
D. revenue stamps affixed to the deed agree with *reported* price

21. The *vesting* date in condemnation cases is the date on which 21.____

    A. a case goes to trial
    B. the owner first makes a claim for his money
    C. the payment of the award is designated by the court
    D. the taking order is signed by the court

22. Depreciation, as the term is used in appraisal literature, USUALLY means a loss in value 22.____

    A. from all causes
    B. from physical deterioration only
    C. from physical deterioration and economic factors only
    D. as certified by a qualified insurance adjuster

23. *Economic Tent* is that rental which is 23.____

    A. reserved in a lease agreement
    B. derived from market data
    C. the average of yearly rentals received during past years
    D. the projected rental expectancy

24. *Effective* rental refers to the 24.____

    A. annualized montly rental now being collected
    B. gross rental expectancy less vacancy allowance
    C. rental stipulated in a lease
    D. base rental plus *overage*

25. The amount of rental income expected to be collected over economic rental is designated as 25.____

    A. overage   B. percentage rental
    C. reserve rental   D. excess rental

26. Office building operational costs are USUALLY expressed in terms of cost per _____ foot. 26.____

    A. gross square   B. cubic
    C. net usable   D. net rentable square

27. The LARGEST single item of operating expense in a modern office building is, generally, 27.____

    A. contractual cleaning
    B. wages (exclusive of cleaning)
    C. oil for heating and cooling
    D. electricity for tenants and buildings

28. The present worth of a net income stream for a period of 15 years deferred five years is the net income multiplied by the _____ factor. 28.____

    A. 20-year   B. 15-year
    C. 20-year factor less the 15-year D. 20-year factor less the 5-year

29. The following formula can be used to develop overall capitalization rate:
R = Y - MC + Depreciation X sinking fund factor
In this formula, the symbol M stands for

A. money
B. mortgage amount
C. mortgage ratio
D. mortgage rate

30. The leased fee position is valued by

A. discounting reserved rentals and adding value of reversion
B. discounting the contract rental stream and adding the present worth of reversion
C. subtracting the present worth of the rental stream from the free-and-clear value of property
D. adding the future value of property to the future value of rental income

31. A title of the administrative code imposes a tax on each deed at the time of delivery of the deed from the grantor to the grantee when the consideration exceeds $250,000. The LEAST valid of the following statements regarding the payment of this transfer tax is that

A. the tax shall be at one-half of one percent of the net consideration
B. a return must be filed either by the grantor or grantee
C. the tax is paid by the grantor but the grantee is liable if the grantor does not pay
D. the grantee, if not otherwise exempt, must pay the tax, if the grantor is exempt

32. Real property owned by senior citizens may be eligible for partial exemption from real estate taxation pursuant to the state real property tax law and the city charter. The one of the following situations which will preclude the granting of the exemption is that the

A. property is owned by husband and wife who are aged 66 and 60 years, respectively
B. combined income of the owners is $24,000 per annum
C. property consists of an owner-occupied legal residence above a grocery store
D. property was acquired less than ten years prior to the date of making application for exemption

33. Pursuant to a section of the real property tax law, new construction deemed eligible for tax exemption benefits by the city during construction and the following four years shall be _____ exempt during the period of construction, followed by _____ of the full assessed valuation.

A. *fully;* two years of exemption at 100% and then two years of exemption at 80%
B. *partially;* two years of exemption at 80% of the full assessed valuation, and an additional two years at 60%
C. *fully;* exemptions of one year at 80%, one year at 60%, one year at 40%, and one year at 20%
D. *fully;* exemptions of one year at 90%, one year at 80%, and two years at 60%

34. An honorably discharged Army Chaplain who is currently ministering to a congregation has applied for a clergyman's exemption and a veteran's exemption on his home. According to the state tax law, this chaplain

   A. cannot get both exemptions on a single piece of property
   B. may be able to get both exemptions but the total exemption is limited to $60,000
   C. may obtain both exemptions if he proves that he resides at the property for which he is claiming exemption
   D. may get both exemptions only if his equity in the house is greater than 30% of its market value

35. The one of the following statements that is VALID with respect to the tax commission is that

   A. the tax commission may place upon the books of the annual record of assessed valuations any omitted parcels prior to the date for public inspection thereof
   B. at least three of the members of the commission must be of a political party different from that of the president of the commission
   C. members of the tax commission have the right of entry upon real property at all reasonable times to ascertain the character of the property
   D. the tax commission may remit or reduce a tax is such tax is found excessive or erroneous within two years after delivery of the assessment rolls to the finance administration for the collection of such tax

36. After a certiorari report has been prepared by an assessor and submitted to the certiorari bureau, he learns that the property has been refinanced.
The one of the following which is the PROPER course of action for an assessor to take in this situation is to

   A. notify the certiorari bureau immediately
   B. note the fact in the field book for future consideration
   C. notify the assessor-in-charge of the county in which the property is located
   D. ignore it as properties are assessed on a free-and-clear basis

37. In order to equalize the tax roll, the finance administrator decides to decrease the assessed value of a parcel of real estate on March 1. The owner has never filed for correction of the valuation.
The finance administrator

   A. must direct the owner to file an application prior to March 15
   B. may make the change on the assessment rolls immediately without notice to the owner
   C. may make the change on the assessment rolls immediately but must give the owner notice prior to March 15
   D. must give the owner ten days' notice prior to making the change

38. An assessor is required to enter certain relevant appraisal data in his field book.
Of the following types of data, the one which he is NOT required to enter in the field book is

   A. zoning designations for each block
   B. gross square foot area and, where appropriate, the cubic content of each building

C. information contained in permits issued by the department of marine and aviation concerning physical improvements to city-owned properties
D. information contained in the city planning commission calendars

39. The one of the following statements that is LEAST valid with regard to property exempted from real property taxes is that

    A. assessors, upon finding a change in either ownership or use for which the exemption was granted, may restore the property to the assessable tax rolls
    B. assessors, upon finding a new improvement on exempt property, must report this fact on a query sheet for referral to the tax commission
    C. if construction has not started on vacant land previously granted tax exemption because of an expressed intention to build upon or develop, the assessor must submit a query sheet for each year that the property remains unimproved
    D. exempt properties of any nature, if wholly exempt, must be assessed on the same basis as taxable realty

40. The landlord's information return, filed with the finance administration, is a(n)

    A. certification of the actual consideration paid for the property by the grantee
    B. valuable source for rental data for commercial properties
    C. statement by the owner of a commercial property that he is not using the structure in violation of zoning use
    D. an architectural computation of the gross square foot area and, where appropriate, the cubic content of a building other than one-family dwellings

KEY (CORRECT ANSWERS)

1.	D	11.	C	21.	D	31.	B
2.	B	12.	B	22.	A	32.	C
3.	B	13.	D	23.	B	33.	A
4.	D	14.	C	24.	B	34.	C
5.	A	15.	C	25.	D	35.	C
6.	A	16.	B	26.	D	36.	C
7.	C	17.	B	27.	A	37.	B
8.	C	18.	A	28.	D	38.	D
9.	D	19.	B	29.	C	39.	A
10.	A	20.	A	30.	B	40.	B

EXAMINATION SECTION
TEST 1

DIRECTIONS: Each question or incomplete statement is followed by several suggested answers or completions. Select the one that BEST answers the question or completes the statement. *PRINT THE LETTER OF THE CORRECT ANSWER IN THE SPACE AT THE RIGHT.*

1. Real property, as legally defined, includes

    A. gas ranges
    B. refrigerators
    C. furniture
    D. heating systems

2. Ownership of real estate includes the exclusive right, in every instance, to

    A. take minerals from the sub-surface portions
    B. receive unobstructed light and air from adjacent parcels
    C. use adjacent parcels for access if the property is land-locked
    D. perpetuate a non-conforming use

3. The *Bundle of Rights* refers to the

    A. constitutional authority to appropriate property
    B. various rights attached to ownership of real estate
    C. rights of tenants under net lease arrangements
    D. sheaf of papers in a real estate transaction

4. Cost equals value when

    A. construction cost indices are stable
    B. national conditions are normal
    C. a new building improves a site most profitably
    D. depreciation is not excessive

5. Market value is BEST defined as the

    A. highest price, expressed in dollars, that a property would sell for under the most favorable market conditions
    B. difference between the Cost Approach and Income Approach
    C. average of the three approaches to Value
    D. highest price, expressed in dollars, that a willing, well-informed buyer would pay and a willing, well-informed seller would accept

6. In order for an object to have value in an economic sense, it MUST have

    A. an attractive appearance
    B. practical utility
    C. a clear title
    D. tangible materials

7. *Highest and Best Use* means

    A. most profitable use
    B. most intensive use
    C. the use which produces the largest dollar income
    D. the largest structure

8. The PROPER point in the appraisal process at which the highest and best use analysis should be made is

   A. correlation of the three approaches
   B. definition of the appraisal problem
   C. final valuation estimate
   D. preliminary survey of the appraisal task

9. The *principle of change* is evidenced in

   A. restrictive covenants running with the land
   B. the evolutionary stages in the life of a neighborhood
   C. the land residual technique
   D. the Sheridan-Karkow formula

10. The *principle of balance* is exhibited in the

    A. process of making adjustments in a market data analysis
    B. refining of the capitalization rate through the utilization of quality considerations on a relative basis
    C. agents in production in a property existing in such relative proportions that they produce the maximum residual net income to land
    D. number of apartments and rooms in an apartment house

11. The *principle of contribution states* that

    A. all three approaches to value contribute equally to the final valuation estimate
    B. land and buildings contribute to the creation of economic rents
    C. the value of an agent in production depends upon how much it adds to net income
    D. only business enterprise makes a real contribution

12. In the cost approach to value, under ideal conditions, land value is estimated by the

    A. analysis of market data on a comparative basis
    B. analysis of local tax assessment records
    C. land residual technique
    D. property residual technique

13. In estimating Replacement Cost, the majority of appraisers use the

    A. quantity survey method
    B. unit cost in place method
    C. ENGINEERING NEWS RECORD
    D. unit cost per cubic or square foot method

14. In the Cost Approach of an appraisal of a parcel of real property, the Replacement Cost estimate should include cost of

    A. wall-to-wall carpeting
    B. insurance during construction of improvements
    C. agent's management fees
    D. washing machines

15. *Accrued Depreciation* is BEST defined as the

    A. provision for recapture of capital invested in improvements on the land
    B. measures taken to guard against excessive decay and physical deterioration
    C. difference between the cost of replacement, new, and the present appraised market value
    D. loss in value resulting from any and all causes

16. In estimating accrued depreciation, it is considered the BEST practice to use

    A. the *observed condition* technique
    B. Age-Life tables
    C. Bureau of Internal Revenue tables
    D. Real Estate Board statistics

17. Only one of the three major components of accrued depreciation is said to result from causes extrinsic to the property being appraised.
    This component is

    A. curable functional obsolescence
    B. physical deterioration
    C. economic obsolescence
    D. incurable functional obsolescence

18. The test to determine whether an item of functional obsolescence is curable or incurable is

    A. the consensus of opinion among real estate brokers
    B. the expenditure required to cure it, an item requiring an expenditure of more than $100,000 being incurable
    C. whether the cost of effecting the cure can be recouped in equivalent or greater value
    D. whether the item is mechanical or structural, the former being curable, the latter incurable

19. A cause of economic obsolescence is

    A. utilization of sub-standard specifications in construction of improvements under appraisal
    B. inadequate electric wiring
    C. poor architectural planning for improvements under appraisal
    D. rent control legislation

20. For purposes of capitalization, net income is USUALLY computed before the expense of

    A. debt service charges   B. property taxes
    C. replacement reserve   D. management

21. Capitalization may be described as

    A. establishing the income to be received
    B. converting the net income into value
    C. computing the amortization on the investment
    D. taking an interest and depreciation return on the building value

4 (#1)

22. The estimate of economic life is based PRIMARILY on the _____ of the improvement. 22.____

   A. physical durability
   B. age
   C. size
   D. relative competitive utility

23. Net income imputable to land is capitalized in perpetuity because 23.____

   A. the entire investment is amortized out of the building income
   B. the land returns are presumed to last forever since urban land does not physically depreciate and land may thus be successively utilized
   C. investors capitalize land income in this manner since they cannot take depreciation on the land for tax purposes
   D. land represents a reversionary interest

24. The capitalization process must provide for recovery of the building investment over the economic life of the building because 24.____

   A. the investment should be recovered at the same approximate rate as the building is anticipated to decline in value from depreciation
   B. it is customary to recover every asset out of income, regardless of whether it is depreciable or not
   C. the investor always believes the amortization on the mortgage is designed to achieve the recovery of his capital for him
   D. amortization may not be equal to depreciation

25. The capitalization process referred to as *direct capitalization plus straight line depreciation* is based on an assumption that the 25.____

   A. income stream will remain level
   B. building has suffered a substantial amount of functional obsolescence
   C. income stream will decline over the years
   D. curing of most accrued depreciation is possible

26. In capitalization techniques, the method of providing for future depreciation that generally permits highest valuation is the 26.____

   A. annuity system
   B. quantity survey
   C. sinking fund
   D. straight line method

27. The building residual technique is applicable when 27.____

   A. accurate building cost data is available
   B. the building improves the site to its highest and best use
   C. land is in short supply in the market
   D. there is an abundance of market data relating to comparable sites

28. A capitalization rate is the 28.____

   A. amount of taxes levied upon a capital gain
   B. equalization rate for property taxes
   C. rate of return necessary to attract capital
   D. rate of capital depreciation

5 (#1)

29. The *Band of Investment* method of selecting a capitalization rate is

   A. built up on the *safe rate*
   B. applicable only when land residual technique will be used
   C. based on analysis of sales
   D. based on weighted average of mortgage and equity rates

30. Since the use of the Inwood (annuity) factor provides for complete depreciation of a real estate investment over its assumed economic life, the use of such technique in the appraisal of improved real property necessitates

   A. provision for substantial tax levies
   B. an estimate of the value of the land reversion
   C. an especially careful neighborhood analysis
   D. a very thorough inspection of improvements

31. In the land residual technique, the appraiser

   A. bases his opinion on careful analysis of market data
   B. need not inspect the building unless there are building violations on it
   C. sometimes bases his estimates on a hypothetical structure representing highest and best use
   D. is concerned only with raw land costs

32. The so-called *overall* capitalization rate is BEST arrived at by

   A. obtaining the ratio of net income to selling price of comparable properties
   B. consulting the Dow Service for the standard capitalization rates most frequently used
   C. examination of Census Statistics
   D. employing the summation or *build-up* technique

33. In real estate appraisal work, the market data approach should particularly be used

   A. when the sales market has experienced substantial activity
   B. when cost information is too difficult to obtain
   C. when the subject property is new
   D. only when a residential property is being appraised

34. The market data approach is used for direct valuation of properties and it is also useful in

   A. making quantity surveys
   B. making insurance appraisals
   C. establishing capitalization rates
   D. controlling depreciation

35. The heart of the market data approach is

   A. thorough checking of deed registration
   B. careful averaging of sales statistics
   C. thorough-going analysis of the records of the Building Department
   D. careful comparisons between comparables and property being appraised

KEY (CORRECT ANSWERS)

1. D
2. A
3. B
4. C
5. D

6. B
7. A
8. D
9. B
10. C

11. C
12. A
13. D
14. B
15. C

16. A
17. C
18. C
19. D
20. A

21. B
22. D
23. B
24. A
25. C

26. A
27. D
28. C
29. D
30. B

31. C
32. A
33. A
34. C
35. D

TEST 2

DIRECTIONS: Each question or incomplete statement is followed by several suggested answers or completions. Select the one that BEST answers the question or completes the statement. *PRINT THE LETTER OF THE CORRECT ANSWER IN THE SPACE AT THE RIGHT.*

1. Appraisals for any purpose in the real estate field, in an economic sense, are required because

    A. a high unit cost is involved
    B. realty is a non-standardized commodity
    C. it is a customary practice
    D. brokers are usually uninformed

    1.____

2. The legal basis for the estimation of full value in real estate tax assessment appraisals is

    A. stabilized market value, without regard to cyclical extremes
    B. a combination of the market comparison and income approaches
    C. cost for improvements, less any depreciation, plus land value estimated by comparison
    D. capitalized value of the residual net income

    2.____

3. In a purely objective sense, no matter what the purpose of the appraisal may be, the market value of the real estate at a given moment is ALWAYS

    A. identical   B. varied
    C. mixed   D. dependent on the approach

    3.____

4. Certiorari appraisals are unique in technique because

    A. they frequently result in court actions
    B. the tax rate is incorporated in the capitalization rate
    C. all three value approaches are used
    D. they are used in no other state except New York

    4.____

5. There is an effective limitation on the height of reinforced concrete structures because

    A. the large columns required take up too much floor space and impair floor layouts
    B. the structural framework is too rigid for climatic changes
    C. the building code limits the height of reinforced concrete structures
    D. it is expensive to haul concrete to excessive heights

    5.____

6. Aside from zoning restrictions, the height of a steel skeleton frame building is limited by the

    A. cost of the steel framing
    B. labor cost involved at great heights resulting from labor scarcity
    C. cost of utility installations
    D. adequacy of the net rent received on the construction cost of the last floor

    6.____

7. A typical semi-fireproof apartment house has

    A. all wood floors but masonry walls
    B. concrete first floor arch, wood upper floors, load bearing masonry walls
    C. light steel bar joists, 2" poured concrete floors, load bearing masonry walls
    D. all concrete floors and load bearing masonry walls

    7.____

8. Continual flaking of paint on the inner surface of an outer masonry wall PROBABLY indicates

   A. a poor paint job caused by adulterating the paint with a chemical
   B. shoddy construction permissible under an inadequate building code
   C. driving rains from the east
   D. a need for pointing up the loose and dislodged mortar in the joints

9. The appraiser makes an inspection of the realty under appraisal because

   A. it keeps him informed on building construction
   B. he must be an engineer to be qualified
   C. the results of the inspection have a direct bearing on the value
   D. a very detailed description of the realty is expected of him

10. The LEAST costly heating system to install and service, which takes the least amount of space and costs the most for fuel, is

    A. coal stoker
    B. oil burner
    C. gas-fired hot water
    D. utility steam

11. The type of material used for plumbing risers, branches, and crotons has a direct bearing on value because

    A. the better the quality and the more durable the material, the higher the anticipated net income
    B. superintendents are prohibited by union rules from making repairs to the plumbing system
    C. the mechanical equipment depreciates in the same manner as the building shell
    D. some types of material become functionally obsolete faster than others

12. An inspection of the rentable space is as important as an inspection of the building shell and equipment because

    A. the appraiser can determine if there are any furnished units
    B. it establishes the basis for a comparable rent analysis
    C. the occupancy must be checked against the leases
    D. it makes the report look more impressive

13. Which one of the following is GENERALLY found in an unaltered old law tenement?

    A. Combination washtub and bathtub
    B. Dumbwaiters
    C. Central heat
    D. Off-foyer layouts

14. Which one of the following is MOST generally found in a new law tenement?

    A. A standpipe system
    B. Dumbwaiters
    C. Colored tile baths
    D. Windowless rooms

15. If an inspection revealed that an apartment house was dangerously underwired, the appraiser should PRIMARILY solve this in his appraisal report by

    A. advising the owner to correct the condition forthwith
    B. advising the client to notify the Building Department immediately
    C. subtracting the capital cost of re-wiring from the market value, after reflecting the rent increases permitted by the Rent Commission in the net income
    D. ignoring the condition on the assumption that the owner will eventually replace the wiring

16. If a building is of competitive, that is, average construction quality, and if it has been well maintained to the date of the appraisal, the LEAST significant type of depreciation is probably

    A. super session B. physical deterioration
    C. functional obsolescence D. inadequacy

17. The type of air conditioning system installed in most new apartment houses is

    A. air-cooled central system with adequate ducts
    B. peripheral system circulating chilled water
    C. heavy duty fan system
    D. unit in wall sleeve

18. Land use is usually the MOST intensive in _____ districts.

    A. apartment B. hotel C. loft D. office

19. A significant decline in employment in a city may affect real estate market values through

    A. economic obsolescence
    B. neighborhood decay
    C. removal of middle class to the suburbs
    D. the aging process

20. The removal of some of the middle income class from the core of the city to the suburbs has resulted in a(n)

    A. increase in the available supply of dwelling units
    B. decline in controlled rents
    C. acceleration of physical deterioration and economic obsolescence in those central residential neighborhoods
    D. opportunity to modernize controlled rent apartments

21. Downtown major retail sections have been adversely affected PRIMARILY by

    A. obsolete buildings
    B. too many taxicabs and too few buses
    C. poor planning of merchant associations
    D. outlying shopping center competition

22. If published material were not available, the BEST source for obtaining the net annual addition to the housing stock would be

    A. condemnation records

B. tax and assessment records
C. the Register's Office
D. building and demolition permits

23. The trend referred to as *decentralization* is caused LARGELY by

    A. encroachment of industry into residential areas in outlying cities throughout the country
    B. rent control legislation
    C. removal of commerce, industry, and people from the heart of the city to outlying cities or to the periphery
    D. inequitable tax assessment policies

24. The cubical content of an office building was 2,100,000 cubic feet. The Dow Service Valuation Calculator gave $1.10 as the net field reproduction cost. The appraiser added 20% to cover all miscellaneous costs and excavation. Depreciation was estimated at 2 1/2% per annum. The building was 25 years old on the appraisal date. Land value was estimated at $15,000 a front foot for the 200' x 100' plot.
    The total value by the cost approach is MOST NEARLY

    A. $4,039,500
    B. $4,762,000
    C. $5,191,300
    D. $6,244,000

25. The quantity survey method of cost estimation is not used by most market value appraisers because

    A. appraisal groups oppose it
    B. they are not qualified to use it
    C. cost has no importance in valuation
    D. the unit-in-place method is better

26. An over-calculation or over-estimation of building cost, assuming a particular level of rent is obtainable, will

    A. influence lenders on the mortgage to require less amortization
    B. penalize the land value by the approximate amount of the over-calculation of the building cost
    C. result in a faulty depreciation allowance for income tax purposes
    D. make necessary the engagement of a cost expert on a sub-contract basis

27. The construction cost of a six-story semi-fireproof apartment house is less than that of a fireproof reinforced concrete apartment house of similar size by APPROXIMATELY

    A. 40%   B. 30%   C. 15%   D. 10%

28. The cost approach can ALWAYS be used in any appraisal because

    A. it can be used as a ceiling of possible market value for the real estate
    B. no appraisal can be made without it
    C. the physical components of realty are the primary bases for market value
    D. it makes the appraisal report more convincing as a result of the cost figures

29. The assessor was assigned to re-appraise for property tax purposes a 60-year-old loft-type structure that was 50% vacant. Many similar structures in the same district had been demolished, and the plots improved with new commercial buildings.
Under the circumstances, which appraisal approach, of the following, would BEST be utilized?

    A. Reproduction cost, less depreciation, plus land value
    B. Replacement cost, plus land value
    C. Market comparison, treating the improvement as almost fully depreciated
    D. the building residual method of capitalization

30. The assessor was assigned to re-appraise for property tax purposes a privately-owned, specially designed and constructed art gallery with high ceilings and ornate construction, for which there was no market in its present use. He concluded that it would not be practical to convert the structure to another use should the art gallery use terminate. He decided to use the cost approach and worked out a reproduction cost for the structure.
In the absence of a market for similar structures, the depreciation computation should MOST probably be based on

    A. May's quantity survey method of computing depreciation
    B. a sinking fund technique
    C. an age-life method based on a straight-line depreciation allowance
    D. an observation derived from personal experience

31. In comparing the results of the cost approach and the income approach when assessing a new building on a given plot, the assessor noted that the income approach yielded a greater total value, despite the use of a high capitalization rate.
Assuming the assessor's cost calculations to be accurate, the differential can BEST be attributed to the fact that

    A. there is always a higher total value when the income approach is used rather than the cost approach
    B. there is usually an increment in value attributable to the land over its acquisition cost, underlying a successfully rented and completed building in a market of equilibrium
    C. the cost approach never reflects the value obtained from the income approach because the former is independent of the rents obtained in the property
    D. the law does not permit equipment in the realty to be treated as real fixtures subject to real estate taxation

32. The assessor was asked to estimate the market land value underlying a one-story store building. The property had recently sold for $1,200,000. The land assessment was $400,000, and the total assessment was $800,000.
Using the assessment ratio extraction process, the assessor should estimate the land value at

    A. $300,000   B. $500,000   C. $600,000   D. $800,000

33. The assessor's unit lot value for a typical side street had been established at $500,000. A vacant corner plot 100' x 75' on the same street sold for $3,000,000. The Hoffman-Neill rule depth factor for 75 feet was 84.49. Assuming standard corner and key lot increments, the unit lot value indicated by the sale is MOST NEARLY

    A. $625,000   B. $700,000   C. $800,000   D. $890,000

34. One of the BEST means of finding the appropriate overall capitalization rate for income property on a market comparison basis is the

    A. earnings price ratio of similar properties
    B. long-term government bond rate in the money market
    C. risk rates in the market
    D. mortgage interest rates

35. You are asked to assess a six-story apartment house on a 100' x 100' plot. You find records of four sales of similar properties.
    Which one has no applicability?

    A. R.S. $.55 mortgage $125,000
    B. R.S. $77. mortgage $80,000 P.M.M. $30,000
    C. R.S. $110. mortgage $65,000
    D. Stated consideration: $1,800,000

KEY (CORRECT ANSWERS)

1. B		16. B
2. C		17. A
3. A		18. D
4. B		19. A
5. A		20. C
6. D		21. D
7. B		22. B
8. D		23. C
9. C		24. A
10. C		25. B
11. A		26. B
12. B		27. C
13. A		28. A
14. B		29. C
15. C		30. C

31. B
32. C
33. B
34. A
35. A

TEST 3

DIRECTIONS: Each question or incomplete statement is followed several suggested answers or completions. Select one that BEST answers the question or completes the statement. *PRINT THE LETTER OF THE CORRECT ANSWER IN THE SPACE AT THE RIGHT.*

1. Which one of the following is an INCORRECT technique for analyzing comparable sales?

    A. Ratio of selling price to assessed valuation
    B. Applying locational differential rating factor
    C. Selling price per unit of measurement
    D. Going back fifteen years in checking sales

    1.____

2. The appraiser employed in a certiorari proceeding submitted twenty-five sales, eighteen of which were made prior to the appraisal date, three within six months after the appraisal date, and the balance two and one-half years after the appraisal date. The MAXIMUM number of sales which the trial justice could admit as evidence of value was

    A. 23   B. 21   C. 19   D. 17

    2.____

3. The market comparison approach is frequently considered the primary or best approach, provided the

    A. income approach is used as a check
    B. subject property is a standardized type and recent comparable market sales are numerous
    C. reproduction cost, less age-life depreciation, plus land value, yields the same result
    D. appraiser subscribes to a sales service

    3.____

4. The assessor was appraising a newly completed apartment house which, in his judgement, was worth less than its replacement cost because of some serious deficiencies in design, layout, and equipment.
In capitalizing the net income, the CORRECT capitalization method to apply to this new building is the _____ method.

    A. building residual   B. land residual
    C. property residual   D. land reversion

    4.____

5. You wish to establish a capitalization rate for the capitalization of net income, before any deduction for depreciation. You decide the Band of Investment Theory is best for this purpose. Debt service charges for similar property is running 8% on a 60% mortgage. Equity returns currently are 10%.
The MOST appropriate capitalization rate is

    A. 7.60%   B. 8.80%   C. 8.90%   D. 9.10%

    5.____

6. Of the following, the BEST mathematical means of capitalizing a net rental from property occupied by an AAA-1 tenant under a thirty year net lease is

    A. annuity table, as Inwood's Premise
    B. interest plus sinking fund
    C. interest plus straight-line depreciation
    D. interest rate, after subtracting depreciation

    6.____

7. The land residual method of capitalization must be used with great caution, particularly when the building has not yet been constructed, because

   A. it requires exceptional technical competence
   B. the leverage factor can produce gross distortions in the residual land return
   C. construction costs are difficult to estimate
   D. it is unethical to capitalize income attributable to a building not yet constructed

8. The method of capitalization which recognizes the valuation principle that land value should never be penalized or discounted merely because of the inadequacy of a depreciated structure is the _____ method.

   A. gross multiplier
   B. net multiplier
   C. building residual
   D. Kniskern-Schmutz

9. Land value under a rent-controlled apartment house was estimated by comparison at $1,000,000. Net income after all expenses except debt service charges was $120,000. The building's economic life was estimated at 25 years and the interest rate at 6%. The annuity factor for 25 years at 6% was 12.78.
   The total value of land and improvements was

   A. $1,766,800
   B. $1,873,600
   C. $2,056,530
   D. $2,593,600

10. The equity return was $4,000. Debt service charges were $6,000. The property sold for $150,000.
    The overall rate of return, free of mortgage debt, was MOST NEARLY

    A. 5.8%   B. 6.2%   C. 6.7%   D. 7.5%

11. The assessor was asked to appraise, for property tax purposes by the property residual method, a department store property under a 40-year lease at $1,000,000 a year. Building life and the lease term are considered coincident. Land value at lease expiration was estimated at $10,000,000. The annuity factor for 40 years at 7% interest was 13.3. The deferment factor for 40 years at 7% interest was .07.
    The present value is MOST NEARLY

    A. $9,800,000
    B. $12,500,000
    C. $13,300,000
    D. $14,000,000

12. A new retail shopping center was considered to represent the highest utilization of the site. It produced a total net income of $1,000,000. The building cost was $8,000,000. Economic life was 40 years. Interest rate was 7%. Assuming straight-line depreciation and employing the most appropriate capitalization methods, the total value is MOST NEARLY

    A. $32,650,000
    B. $26,300,000
    C. $21,250,000
    D. $11,430,000

13. For the property in the preceding question, the ratio of land to total appraised value is MOST NEARLY

    A. 20%   B. 30%   C. 40%   D. 50%

14. You are appraising a vacant lot 25' x 75', 25' from the corner.
    Which of the following would you consider in estimating the size of the unit lot?

    A. Corner influence, plus Hoffman-Neill factor
    B. Corner and key influence
    C. Key influence, plus Hoffman-Neill factor
    D. Key influence

15. The RECORD AND GUIDE reported the following sale: Park Ave., 908-910 (5:149-37 swc, 80th (Nos. 70-76) 81.2 x 80.6, 14 sty. apt; Harry and Jane Fischel Foundation (Albert Wald, v.pres.) 960 Park Ave. to 910 Park Ave., Inc. 910 Park Ave.; B&S; 1st mtg. $165,734.19; PM mtge. $489,151.08; Apr. 30; May 2 '57; A $235,000. $470,000 (RS $725.45).
    What is the selling price and cash payment, respectively?

    A. $825,234.19; $170,348.12
    B. $1,413,583.72; $569,250.00
    C. $319,681.41; $320,281.00
    D. $975,432.00; $251,684.44

16. Using the sales figures given in the preceding question and assuming the depth factor for 80' is 87.73, the number of unit lots and the unit lot value, respectively, are MOST NEARLY _____ unit lots and _____.

    A. 3.27; $78,904.00
    B. 3.69; $91,283.00
    C. 3.92; $69,524.00
    D. 3.72; $111,130.00

17. According to the Tax Department, the assessor's field book must contain

    A. notations on national real estate conditions for each tax year
    B. annuity tables pasted on the inside fold
    C. the actual condition of all buildings in course of construction as of taxable status date
    D. the telephone numbers of taxpayers

18. The CHIEF function of the Tax Department's Research Bureau is to

    A. engage in primary research in real estate, economics, and valuation techniques
    B. prepare research reports for the City Planning Commission
    C. tabulate the ratio of selling prices to assessed values in various cities throughout the country
    D. act as an adjunct of the Certiorari Bureau

19. The property cards furnished each assessor do NOT contain

    A. sales and leases
    B. court decisions
    C. construction costs
    D. national real estate market index

20. Which one of the following is NOT entitled to partial or complete tax exemption?

    A. Medical society
    B. Parsonages
    C. Trade association
    D. Veterans' organization

21. In New York City, exempt property is MOST NEARLY what percent of the total of all property?

    A. 15%   B. 25%   C. 30%   D. 35%

22. The *Assessor's Report for Certiorari Hearing,* in addition to providing a detailed physical description, also computes

    A. the capitalization of the income
    B. the percent of net on the assessed value
    C. the operating costs per cubic foot
    D. a quantity survey cost estimate

23. An example of a typical expense usually listed under Item 9, OTHER EXPENSES, in an Application for Correction of Assessed Valuation of Real Estate is

    A. hall and corridor painting
    B. plumbing repairs
    C. liability insurance
    D. management fees

24. In connection with an Application for Additional Veteran Exemption, the item of information which the assessor must obtain is the

    A. cost of capital improvements to property since purchase
    B. quantity survey cost estimates from reliable contractors
    C. type of veteran's discharge
    D. date on which the veteran purchased the property

25. A remission of real estate from taxation occasionally occurs when

    A. a corporation has a foreign charter
    B. taxes have been in arrears for three or more years
    C. an *in rem* proceeding is pending
    D. a corporation qualifies for tax exemption

KEY (CORRECT ANSWERS)

1. D
2. B
3. B
4. A
5. B

6. A
7. B
8. C
9. A
10. C

11. D
12. D
13. B
14. C
15. A

16. D
17. C
18. A
19. D
20. C

21. C
22. B
23. D
24. A
25. D

EXAMINATION SECTION
TEST 1

DIRECTIONS: Each question or incomplete statement is followed by several suggested answers or completions. Select the one that BEST answers the question or completes the statement. *PRINT THE LETTER OF THE CORRECT ANSWER IN THE SPACE AT THE RIGHT.*

1. When a supervisor requests a subordinate to prepare a report, he should not only indicate the areas to be covered in the report but should also indicate to the subordinate

    A. for whom it is intended and its purpose
    B. the conclusions he expects to reach
    C. the decision that he will make based on the facts presented
    D. why that subordinate was chosen to prepare it

    1.____

2. The MOST accurate of the following principles of education and learning for a supervisor to keep in mind when planning a training program for the assistant supervisors under her supervision is that

    A. assistant supervisors, like all other individuals, vary in the rate at which they learn new material and in the degree to which they can retain what they do learn
    B. experienced assistant supervisors who have the same basic college education and agency experience will be able to learn new material at approximately the same rate of speed
    C. the speed with which assistant supervisors can learn new material after the age of forty is half as rapid as at ages twenty to thirty
    D. with regard to any specific task, it is easier and takes less time to break an experienced assistant supervisor of old, unsatisfactory work habits than it is to teach him new, acceptable ones

    2.____

3. Assume that you are a supervisor and that you are planning to train a group of experienced investigators in certain specific skills which they need in their daily work.
   The one of the following methods which may *generally* be expected to be MOST valuable in ascertaining the effectiveness of the training program is to

    A. administer an objective examination to these investigators prior to conducting the training program and an equivalent form of the examination after the program and compare the results
    B. evaluate and compare the work records of these investigators with regard to these skills prior to and after completion of the training program
    C. hold a staff meeting with the investigators after the training program is completed and allow them to discuss frankly their opinions of the values they derived from the various parts of the training
    D. prepare an objective and detailed questionnaire covering the program, have the investigators answer without identifying themselves, and analyze the answers given

    3.____

4. A supervisor has received orders for a work assignment to be carried out by his unit. He has firmly decided on methods for carrying out this assignment which he believes will lead to its completion both properly and expeditiously. He has no intention whatsoever of changing his mind. After he has reached his decision, he calls a staff conference to discuss various alternative methods of carrying out the assignments without making clear that he has already decided upon the method to be used.
To hold a conference of this type would GENERALLY be a

   A. *good* idea, ecause his subordinates are likely to carry the assignment through better if they believe that they devised the methods used
   B. *good* idea, because the staff will have the opportunity and be properly motivated to gain knowledge and experience in methodology without endangering staff performance
   C. *poor* idea, because it would be a failure on the part of the supervisor to show the firm leadership which his unit has a right to expect
   D. *poor* idea, because the discovery by the staff that they had not actually participated in deciding upon methods to be used would have an adverse effect upon their morale

5. Supervisors are frequently faced with the necessity of training old employees in new tasks. An employee inexperienced in a task is much more likely to make a mistake than one who is experienced in it.
In delegating authority to an old employee to perform a new task, a supervisor should GENERALLY

   A. delegate the authority as soon as the subordinate gains minimum competence, allowing him to make mistakes which will not do major damage to the client or to the agency program
   B. delegate the authority as soon as the subordinate gains minimum competence but supervise him closely, enough so that he will not have the opportunity to make even minor mistakes
   C. make the delegation of authority dependent upon the importance which the client places upon the problems involved
   D. withhold the authority until the employee has become experienced in performing the task

6. A supervisor has been transferred from supervision of one group of units to another group of units. She spends the first three weeks in her new assignment in getting acquainted with her new subordinates, their problems, and their work. In this process, she notices that some of the records and forms which are submitted to her by two of the assistant supervisors are carelessly or improperly prepared.
The BEST of the following actions for the supervisor to take in this situation is to

   A. carefully check the work submitted by these assistant supervisors during an additional three weeks before taking any more positive action
   B. confer with these offending workers and show each one where her work needs improvement and how to go about achieving it
   C. institute an in-service training program specifically designed to solve such a problem and instruct the entire subordinate staff in proper work methods
   D. make a note of these errors for documentary use in preparing the annual service rating reports and advise the workers involved to prepare their work more carefully

7. A supervisor, who was promoted to this position a year ago, has supervised a certain assistant supervisor for this one year. The work of the assistant supervisor has been very poor because he has done a minimum of work, refused to take sufficient responsibility, been difficult to handle, and required very close supervision. Apparently due to the increasing insistence by his supervisor that he improve the caliber of his work, the assistant supervisor tenders his resignation, stating that the demands of the job are too much for him. The opinion of the previous supervisor, who had supervised this assistant supervisor for two years, agrees substantially with that of the new supervisor. Under such circumstances, the BEST of the following actions the supervisor can take in general is to

   A. recommend that the resignation be accepted and that he be rehired should he later apply when he feels able to do the job
   B. recommend that the resignation be accepted and that he not be rehired should he later so apply
   C. refuse to accept the resignation but try to persuade the assistant supervisor to accept psychiatric help
   D. refuse to accept the resignation, promising the assistant supervisor that he will be less closely supervised in the future since he is now so experienced

8. After completing a conference with a supervisor concerning the ramifications of a complex problem, an employee informs the supervisor that she feels that her assistant supervisor is too strict in her handling of all the workers under her supervision, especially in comparison with the other assistant supervisors.
   The one of the following actions which is *generally* BEST for the supervisor to take is to

   A. advise the worker in a friendly fashion to apply for a transfer to a unit which has a more lenient supervisor
   B. caution the employee that complaining about a fellow employee behind her back is frowned upon by higher authority as it is a sign of disloyalty
   C. inform the employee that she, the supervisor, will investigate the complaint to determine whether or not it has any validity
   D. tell the worker that the closer and stricter a supervisor is, the better and more completely trained will be her subordinate staff

9. Rumors have arisen to the effect that one of the investigators under your supervision has been attending classes at a local university during afternoon hours when he is supposed to be making field visits.
   The BEST of the following ways for you to approach this problem is to

   A. disregard the rumors since, like most rumors, they probably have no actual foundation in fact
   B. have a discreet investigation made in order to determine the actual facts prior to taking any other action
   C. inform the investigator that you know what he has been doing and that such behavior is overt dereliction of duty and is punishable by dismissal
   D. review the investigator's work record, spot check his performance, and take no further action unless the quality of his work is below average for the unit

10. A supervisor must consider many factors in evaluating a worker whom he has supervised for a considerable time. In evaluating the capacity of such a worker to use independent judgment, the one of the following to which the supervisor should *generally* give MOST consideration is the worker's

A. capacity to establish good relationships with people (clients, colleagues)
B. educational background
C. emotional stability
D. the quality and judgment shown by the worker in previous work situations known to the supervisor

11. A supervisor is conducting a special meeting with the assistant supervisors under her supervision to read and discuss some major complex changes in the rules and procedures. She notices that one of the assistant supervisors who is normally attentive at meetings seems to be paying no attention to what is being said. The supervisor stops reading the rules and asks the assistant supervisor a couple of questions about the changed procedure, to which she gets satisfactory answers.
The BEST action of the following for the supervisor to take at the meeting is to

   A. advise the assistant supervisor gently but firmly that these changes are complex and that her undivided attention is required in order to fully comprehend them
   B. avoid further embarrassment to the assistant supervisor by asking the group as a whole to pay more attention to what is being read
   C. discontinue the questioning and resume reading the procedure
   D. politely request the assistant supervisor to stop giving those present the impression that she is uninterested in what goes on about her

12. A supervisor becomes aware that one of her very competent experienced workers never takes notes during an interview with a client except to note an occasional name, address, or date. When asked about this practice by the supervisor, the worker states that she has a good memory for important details and has always been able to satisfactorily record an interview after the client has left.
It would *generally* be BEST for the supervisor to handle this situation by

   A. discussing with her that more extensive note-taking may sometimes be desirable with a client who believes note-taking to be evidence that his problem will receive serious consideration
   B. agreeing with this practice since note-taking interferes with the establishment of a proper worker-client relationship
   C. explaining that, since interviewing is an art form rather than an exact science, a good worker must devise her own personal rules for interviewing and not be bound by general principles
   D. warning the worker that memory is too uncertain a thing to be relied upon and, therefore, notes should be taken during an interview of all matters

13. When an experienced subordinate who has the authority and information necessary to make a decision on a certain difficult matter brings the matter to his supervisor without having made the decision, it would *generally* be BEST for the supervisor to

   A. agree to make the decision for the subordinate after the subordinate has explained why he finds it difficult to make the decision and after he has made a recommendation
   B. make the decision for the subordinate, explaining to him the reasons for arriving at the decision
   C. refuse to make the decision, but discuss the various alternatives with the subordinate in order to clarify the issues involved
   D. refuse to make the decision, explaining to the subordinate that he is deemed to be fully qualified and competent to make the decision

14. The one of the following instances when it is MOST important for an upper-level supervisor to follow the chain of command is when he is

    A. communicating decisions
    B. communicating information
    C. receiving suggestions
    D. seeking information

15. Experts in the field of personnel relations feel that it is generally a bad practice for subordinate employees to become aware of pending or contemplated changes in policy or organizational set-up via the *grapevine* CHIEFLY because

    A. evidence that one or more responsible officials have proved untrustworthy will undermine confidence in the agency
    B. the information disseminated by this method is seldom entirely accurate and generally spreads needless unrest among the subordinate staff
    C. the subordinate staff may conclude that the administration feels the staff cannot be trusted with the true information
    D. the subordinate staff may conclude that the administration lacks the courage to make an unpopular announcement through official channels

16. In order to maintain a proper relationship with a worker who is assigned to staff rather than line functions, a line supervisor should

    A. accept all recommendations of the staff worker
    B. include the staff worker in the conferences called by the supervisor for his subordinates
    C. keep the staff worker informed of developments in the area of his staff assignment
    D. require that the staff worker's recommendations be communicated to the supervisor through the supervisor's own superior

17. Of the following, the GREATEST disadvantage of placing a worker in a staff position under the direct supervision of the supervisor whom he advises is the possibility that the

    A. staff worker will tend to be insubordinate because of a feeling of superiority over the supervisor
    B. staff worker will tend to give advice of the type which the supervisor wants to hear or finds acceptable
    C. supervisor will tend to be mistrustful of the advice of a worker of subordinate rank
    D. supervisor will tend to derive little benefit from the advice because to supervise properly he should know at least as much as his subordinate

18. One factor which might be given consideration in deciding upon the optimum span of control of a supervisor over his immediate subordinates is the position of the supervisor in the hierarchy of the organization.
    It is GENERALLY considered proper that the number of subordinates immediately supervised by a higher, upper echelon supervisor

    A. is unrelated to and tends to form no pattern with the number supervised by lower-level supervisors
    B. should be about the same as the number supervised by a lower-level supervisor
    C. should be larger than the number supervised by a lower-level supervisor
    D. should be smaller than the number supervised by a lower-level supervisor

19. An important administrative problem is how precisely to define the limits on authority that is delegated to subordinate supervisors.
Such definition of limits of authority should be

    A. as precise as possible and practicable in all areas
    B. as precise as possible and practicable in areas of function, but should allow considerable flexibility in the area of personnel management
    C. as precise as possible and practicable in the area of personnel management, but should allow considerable flexibility in the areas of function
    D. in general terms so as to allow considerable flexibility both in the areas of function and in the areas of personnel management

19._____

20. The LEAST important of the following reasons why a particular activity should be assigned to a unit which performs activities dissimilar to it is that

    A. close coordination is needed between the particular activity and other activities performed by the unit
    B. it will enhance the reputation and prestige of the unit supervisor
    C. the unit makes frequent use of the results of this particular activity
    D. the unit supervisor has a sound knowledge and understanding of the particular activity

20._____

21. In a conference on difficult cases between a recently appointed supervisor and an experienced, above-average employee, the MOST valuable of the following services that the supervisor can offer the employee is a

    A. detached point of view
    B. knowledge of human needs
    C. knowledge of the agency's basic rules and regulations
    D. willingness to make decisions

21._____

22. A supervisor is put in charge of a special unit. She is exceptionally well qualified for this assignment by her training and experience. One of her very close personal friends has been working for some time in this unit. Both the supervisor and worker are certain that the rest of the employees in the unit, many of whom have been in the bureau for a long time, know of this close relationship.
Under these circumstances, the MOST advisable action for the supervisor to take is to

    A. ask that either she be allowed to return to her old assignment or, if that cannot be arranged, that her friend be transferred to another unit in the center
    B. avoid any overt sign of favoritism by acting impartiall and with greater reserve when dealing with this employee than with the rest of the staff
    C. discontinue any socializing with this employee either inside or outside the office so as to eliminate any gossip or dissatisfaction
    D. talk the situation over with the employee and arrive at a mutually acceptable plan of proper office decorum

22._____

23. A supervisor who wishes to attain established objectives should concentrate on

    A. determining whether management is operating at maximum effectiveness
    B. making suggestions for improving the organization
    C. planning work assignments
    D. securing salary increases for needy employees

23._____

24. A usually competent employee complains that he does not understand the procedures to be followed in performing a certain task although the supervisor has explained them twice and has demonstrated them.
Of the following, the BEST course of action for the supervisor to take is to

   A. ask the employee whether he has any problems which are bothering him
   B. assign someone else to the job
   C. explain the procedures again and demonstrate at the same time
   D. have the employee perform the job while he watches and gives additional instructions

25. GENERALLY, in order to be completely qualified as a supervisor, a person

   A. should be able to perform exceptionally well at least one of the jobs he supervises and have some knowledge of the others
   B. must have an intimate working knowledge of all facets of the jobs which he supervises
   C. should know the basic principles and procedures of the jobs he supervises
   D. need know little or nothing of the jobs which he supervises as long as he knows the principles of supervision

KEY (CORRECT ANSWERS)

1. A	11. C
2. A	12. A
3. B	13. C
4. D	14. A
5. A	15. B
6. B	16. C
7. B	17. B
8. C	18. D
9. B	19. A
10. D	20. B

21. A
22. A
23. C
24. D
25. C

TEST 2

DIRECTIONS: Each question or incomplete statement is followed by several suggested answers or completions. Select the one that BEST answers the question or completes the statement. *PRINT THE LETTER OF THE CORRECT ANSWER IN THE SPACE AT THE RIGHT.*

1. Your superior has asked you to notify employees of an important change in one of the operating procedures described in the manual. Every employee presently has a copy of this manual.
   Which of the following is *normally* the MOST practical way to get the employees to understand such a change?

   A. Notify each employee individually of the change and answer any questions he might have
   B. Send a written notice to key personnel, directing them to inform the people under them
   C. Call a general meeting, distribute a corrected page for the manual, and discuss the change
   D. Send a memo to employees describing the change in general terms and asking them to make the necessary corrections in their copies of the manual

   1.____

2. A supervisor was directed by the head of his division to report figures for overtime wages. The supervisor asked a clerk under his supervision to give him the figures, and he passed the clerk's figures along to his superior without questioning them. It was then discovered that the clerk had carelessly supplied the wrong information. Who can PROPERLY be held responsible for the mistake, the supervisor or the payroll clerk?

   A. Only the supervisor because he should have known that the clerk would be careless
   B. Only the clerk because it should be unnecessary for supervisors to check the work of their subordinates except for work which is unusually complex or important
   C. Neither of them because it is perfectly understandable that such mistakes will occur from time to time
   D. Both of them because the person to whom a task is delegated is responsible to the supervisor who delegated the task, and the supervisor is responsible to his superior

   2.____

3. As a supervisor, it is necessary for you to show a new employee how to enter information on standard forms that he will have to prepare. These forms have a number of blanks to be filled in, but the job is fairly simple once a person becomes familiar with it.
   The BEST way to show the new employee how to do the job is to

   A. explain how to do it and have him fill out a few forms, helping him with any difficulties
   B. give him a completed form to use as a model and tell him to do all the others exactly the same way
   C. put him on his own immediately and assume that he will learn for himself through trial and error
   D. give him several dozen completed forms to read and ask him to check back with you in a few hours when he feels ready to start work

   3.____

4. Suppose that a usually competent employee whom you supervise has suddenly begun having difficulty completing his assignments. You ask the employee to speak to you privately about this situation, and he agrees that he would appreciate this opportunity because of a problem he is having.
Of the following, which one would be the BEST technique for you to use in speaking with him?

   A. Criticize the employee's performance as soon as he mentions his difficulty in completing his assignments
   B. Listen patiently to what the employee has to say before making any comments on your own
   C. Refuse to discuss any personal factors which the employee mentions when he tries to explain his recent work difficulty
   D. Allow the employee to argue with you but plan your attack and defense carefully

5. A certain supervisor does not compliment members of his staff when they come up with good ideas. He feels that coming up with good ideas is part of the job and does not merit special attention.
This supervisor's practice is

   A. *poor,* because recognition for good ideas is a good motivator
   B. *poor,* because the staff will suspect that the supervisor has no good ideas of his own
   C. *good,* because it is reasonable to assume that employees will tell their supervisor of ways to improve office practice
   D. *good,* because the other members of the staff are not made to seem inferior by comparison

6. An employee under your supervision complains about a decision you have made in assigning work in the office. You consider the matter to be unimportant, but it seems to be very important to him. He is excited and very angry. Of the following, the MOST appropriate action for you to take FIRST is to

   A. listen to the details of his complaint
   B. refer him to your superior
   C. tell him to *cool off* before discussing the matter
   D. tell him to settle it with the other employees

7. An experienced employee complains to his unit supervisor that the latter's continual, very close supervision of his work is unnecessary and annoying. The unit supervisor has been recently appointed.
Of the following, it would *generally* be BEST for the unit supervisor to

   A. agree to discontinue all supervision if the employee will agree, if he has any problems, to consult the supervisor
   B. assure the employee that close supervision is necessary but should not be taken personally
   C. consider with the employee what aspects of the supervision could be reduced
   D. explain that he is supervising closely only until he learns what the job is all about

8. A supervisor had a clerk assigned to help him review records. One day the supervisor asked the clerk to continue checking the records, and the clerk said, *No, I'm not doing any more of that today.*
   In this instance, the supervisor should IMMEDIATELY

   A. ask the clerk why he will not check the records
   B. ask another clerk to do the job
   C. tell the clerk he must do it or be transferred
   D. contact his own supervisor

8.____

9. Assume that you have been assigned to supervise other employees. You find that one of your subordinates makes many mistakes whenever he prepares a particular report. Of the following, the MOST desirable course of action for you to follow FIRST in such a situation is to

   A. retrain the subordinate in the preparation of the report
   B. transfer the subordinate to another unit
   C. tell the subordinate to improve or resign
   D. give the employee different duties

9.____

10. Some employees of a department have sent an anonymous letter containing many complaints to the department head. Of the following, what is this MOST likely to show about the department?

    A. It is probably a good place to work.
    B. Communications are probably poor.
    C. The complaints are probably unjustified.
    D. These employees are probably untrustworthy.

10.____

11. Of the following, the BEST reason for rotating employee work assignments is that such rotation

    A. challenges the ingenuity of supervisors in making assignments
    B. gives each employee a chance at both desirable and undesirable assignments
    C. creates specialists among all employees
    D. increases the competitive spirit among employees

11.____

12. Although an employee under your supervision frequently protests when receiving a monotonous assignment, he nevertheless performs the assigned task efficiently. His protests, however, disturb the other employees and interfere with their work.
    Of the following actions you may take in handling this employee, the MOST desirable one is for you to

    A. point out to him the effect of his conduct on the staff's work and request his cooperation in accepting such assignments
    B. arrange to issue such assignments to him when the other members of the staff are not present
    C. inform him that you will request his transfer to another unit unless he puts a halt to his unjustifiable protests
    D. ask other members of the staff to tell him that he is disturbing them by his protests

12.____

13. A supervisor has had several problems with a clerk who assists him. He calls the clerk in for a discussion of the matters.
    Which of the following should comprise the MAJOR part of the discussion?

    A. All the things the clerk has done wrong
    B. The most recent things the clerk has done wrong
    C. The things the clerk has done well in addition to the things he has done wrong
    D. The clerk's previous experience and personal problems

14. Assume that certain work processed in your office is then sent to another office for further processing. One of the employees in your office tells you that the supervisor in the other office has been complaining about your office's method of handling the work.
    Of the following, the MOST appropriate action for you to take is to

    A. get all the details from the employee and then speak to the other supervisor
    B. ignore the situation and continue to do the best you can
    C. remind the supervisor that it is not his function to evaluate your work
    D. refrain from reporting the matter to your superior

15. It is the practice in your department to make objective evaluations of the performance of different units. This requires looking at the results achieved by a particular unit during a specified period of time; for instance, the number of applications processed, the number of inquiries answered, the number of inspections made, and so forth.
    Of the following, the BEST method of evaluating the performance of each unit is to compare its results with the

    A. results achieved by all units of the same size that are performing other kinds of work
    B. goals that the unit was reasonably expected to meet during the specified period
    C. performance of the same unit during a similar period of time four or five years earlier
    D. amount of money spent to achieve these results

16. It is possible that you may be asked to submit a brief written evaluation of the work of several employees under your supervision.
    Such an evaluation should *normally* give LEAST emphasis to an employee's

    A. attendance record, including tardiness and absence
    B. ability to grasp new assignments and carry them out effectively
    C. educational background and previous employment experience
    D. ability to get along with co-workers

17. Of the following leadership characteristics, the one that is *generally* considered PRIMARY for a supervisor is the ability to

    A. achieve good working relations with fellow supervisors
    B. get subordinates to air their personal problems
    C. take action to get the job done
    D. plan his work efficiently

18. A recently appointed supervisor is placed in charge of a district which includes several senior employees. He finds that while these subordinates are able to learn new tasks and methods, some of them tend to take longer to learn procedural changes than newer, younger workers.
Of the following, the MAIN reason for this is that senior workers

    A. are embarrassed by younger workers' intelligence
    B. have to *unlearn* what was taught them in the past
    C. form learning blocks when they are supervised by a younger person
    D. are more interested in doing the work than in academic discussions

18.____

19. Which of the following is *generally* considered to be the MOST desirable way for a supervisor to begin a discussion of an employee's performance with the employee?

    A. Accentuate the positive by giving credit where credit is due
    B. Encourage the employee to suggest ways in which he can improve
    C. Point out specific instances of poor performance
    D. Suggest training programs that the employee may be interested in

19.____

20. For a supervisor to use consultative supervision with his subordinates effectively, it is ESSENTIAL that he

    A. accept the fact that his formal authority will be weakened by the procedure
    B. admit that he does not know more than all his men together and that his ideas are not always best
    C. utilize a committee system so that the procedure is orderly
    D. make sure that all subordinates are consulted so that no one feels left out

20.____

21. During a conversation with his supervisor, a subordinate begins to discuss what appears to the supervisor to be a deep-seated personality problem that has been bothering the subordinate.
For the supervisor to suggest to the subordinate the possibility of professional help would NORMALLY be

    A. *undesirable;* the necessity of requiring professional help would automatically disqualify the subordinate from being promoted in the future
    B. *desirable;* generally a supervisor can be of limited assistance in personally solving deep-seated personality problems
    C. *undesirable;* since the supervisor was approached by the employee, it is his responsibility as a supervisor to help the employee solve his problem
    D. *desirable;* in accordance with the Civil Service Commission regulations, a supervisor is not allowed to get involved in subordinates' personal problems

21.____

22. When a new method of performing a job operation is to be instituted, the one of the following approaches which will MOST generally gain acceptance of the change by subordinates is to

    A. hold a friendly, informal meeting after the change has been implemented to explain the advantages of the new method
    B. consult the subordinates involved in the change as early as possible in the planning stage
    C. work closely with just one of the subordinates who will be affected by the change so that others need not be taken off the job

22.____

D. implement the change, instruct employees fully in the new method, and then follow up on results

23. Of the following, the supervisory practice which is LEAST likely to produce a favorable work environment is that the supervisor   23._____

    A. takes an active interest in subordinates
    B. does not tolerate mistakes, regardless of who has made the mistake
    C. gives praise when justified
    D. disciplines individuals in accordance with their violation of the rules

24. When a supervisor finds it necessary to let a subordinate know that he is dissatisfied with the subordinate's level of performance, which of the following tactics would *usually* prove MOST effective in improving the subordinate's performance?   24._____

    A. The supervisor should be angry when criticizing in order to prevent the mistakes from recurring.
    B. Once criticism has been made, the supervisor should be sure to continuously impress the seriousness of the mistakes upon the subordinate.
    C. When making his criticism, the supervisor should guard against referring to any work that was well done since this would reduce the effect of his criticism.
    D. The supervisor should focus his criticism on the mistakes being made and should avoid downgrading the subordinate personally.

25. Of the following, the BEST descriptive statement of an effective supervisor is *generally* that he   25._____

    A. works alongside his subordinates on the same type of work
    B. catches all errors when they are made
    C. gives many specific work orders and few general work orders
    D. devotes much of his time to long-range activities, such as planning and improving human relations

KEY (CORRECT ANSWERS)

1. C
2. D
3. A
4. B
5. A

6. A
7. C
8. A
9. A
10. B

11. B
12. A
13. C
14. A
15. B

16. C
17. C
18. B
19. A
20. D

21. B
22. B
23. B
24. D
25. D

———

EXAMINATION SECTION
TEST 1

DIRECTIONS: Each question or incomplete statement is followed by several suggested answers or completions. Select the one that BEST answers the question or completes the statement. *PRINT THE LETTER OF THE CORRECT ANSWER IN THE SPACE AT THE RIGHT.*

1. The one of the following which is the CHIEF reason for the difference between the administration of justice agencies and that of other units in public administration is that

    A. correctional institutions are concerned with security
    B. some defendants are proven to be innocent after trial
    C. the administration of justice is much more complicated than other aspects of public administration
    D. correctional institutions produce services their *clients* or *customers* fail to understand or ask for

2. Of the following, the MOST important reason why employees resist change is that

    A. they have not received adequate training in preparation for the change
    B. experience has shown that when new ideas don't work, employees get blamed and not the individuals responsible for the new ideas
    C. new ideas and methods almost always represent a threat to the security of the individuals involved
    D. new ideas often are not practical and disrupt operations unnecessarily

3. Stress situations are ideal for building up a backlog of knowledge about an employee's behavior. Not only does it inform the supervisor of many aspects of a person's behavior patterns, but it is also vitally important to have foreknowledge of how people behave under stress.
    The one of the following which is NOT implied by this passage is that

    A. a person under stress may give some indication of his unsuitability for work in an institution
    B. putting people under stress is the best means of determining their usual patterns of behavior
    C. stress situations may give important clues about performance in the service
    D. there is a need to know about a person's reaction to situations *when the chips are down*

4. There are situations requiring a supervisor to give direct orders to subordinates assigned to work under the direct control of other supervisors.
    Under which of the following conditions would this shift of command responsibility be MOST appropriate?

    A. Emergency operations require the cooperative action of two or more organizational units.
    B. One of the other supervisors is not doing his job, thus defeating the goals of the organization.
    C. The subordinates are performing their assigned tasks in the absence of their own supervisor.
    D. The subordinates ask a superior officer who is not their own supervisor how to perform an assignment given them by their supervisor.

5. The one of the following which BEST differentiates staff supervision from line supervision is that

   A. staff supervision has the authority to immediately correct a line subordinate's action
   B. staff supervision is an advisory relationship
   C. line supervision goes beyond the normal boundaries of direct supervision within a *command*
   D. line supervision does not report findings and make recommendations

6. Decision-making is a rational process calling for a *suspended judgment* by the supervisor until all the facts have been ascertained and analyzed, and the consequences of alternative courses of action studied; *then* the decision maker

   A. acts as both judge and jury and selects what he believes to be the best of the alternative plans
   B. consults with those who will be most directly involved to obtain a recommendation as to the most appropriate course of action
   C. reviews the facts which he has already analyzed, reduces his thoughts to writing, and selects that course of action which can have the fewest negative consequences if his thinking contains an error
   D. stops, considers the matter for at least a 24-hour period, before referring it to a superior for evaluation

7. Decision-making can be defined as the

   A. delegation of authority and responsibility to persons capable of performing their assigned duties with moderate or little supervision
   B. imposition of a supervisor's decision upon a work group
   C. technique of selecting the course of action with the most desired consequences, and the least undesired or unexpected consequences
   D. process principally concerned with improvement of procedures

8. A supervisor who is not well-motivated and has no desire to accept basic responsibilities will

   A. compromise to the extent of permitting poor performance for lengthy periods without correction
   B. get good performance from his work group if the employees are satisfied with their pay and other working conditions
   C. not have marginal workers in his work group if the work is interesting
   D. perform adequately as long as the work of his group consists of routine operations

9. A supervisor is more than a bond or connecting link between two levels of employees. He has joint responsibility which must be shared with both management and with the work group.
Of the following, the item which BEST expresses the meaning of this statement is:

   A. A supervisor works with both management and the work group and must reconcile the differences between them.
   B. In management, the supervisor is solely concerned with efforts directing the work of his subordinates.
   C. The supervisory role is basically that of a liaison man between management and the work force.
   D. What a supervisor says and does when confronted with day-to-day problems depends upon his level in the organization.

10. Operations research is the observation of operations in business or government, and it utilizes both hypotheses and controlled experiments to determine the outcome of decisions. In effect, it reproduces the future impact on the decision in a clinical environment suited to intensive study.
Operations research has

   A. been more promising than applied research in the ascertaining of knowledge for the purpose of decision-making
   B. never been amenable to fact analysis on the grand scale
   C. not been used extensively in government
   D. proven to be the only rational and logical approach to decision-making on long-range problems

11. Assume that a civilian makes a complaint regarding the behavior of a certain worker to the supervisor of the worker. The supervisor regards the complaint as unjustified and unreasonable.
In these circumstances, the supervisor

   A. must make a written note of the complaint and forward it through channels to the unit or individual responsible for complaint investigations
   B. should assure the complainant that disciplinary action will be appropriate to the seriousness of the alleged offense
   C. should immediately summon the worker if he is available so that the latter may attempt to straighten out the difficulty
   D. should inform the complainant that his complaint appears to be unjustified and unreasonable

12. Modern management usually establishes a personal history folder for an employee at the time of hiring. Disciplinary matters appear in such personal history folders. Employees do not like the idea of disciplinary actions appearing in their permanent personal folders.
Authorities believe that

   A. after a few years have passed since the commission of the infraction, disciplinary actions should be removed from folders
   B. disciplinary actions should remain in folders; it is not the records but the use of records that requires detailed study
   C. most personnel have not had disciplinary action taken against them and would resent the removal of disciplinary actions from such folders
   D. there is no point in removing disciplinary actions from personal history folders since employees who have been guilty of infractions should not be allowed to forget their infractions

13. While supervisors should not fear the acceptance of responsibility, they

    A. generally seek out responsibility that subordinates should exercise, particularly when the supervisors do not have sufficient work to do
    B. must be on guard against the abuse of authority that often accompanies the acceptance of total responsibility
    C. should avoid responsibility that is customarily exercised by their superiors
    D. who are anxious for promotions accept responsibility but do not exercise the authority warranted by the responsibility

14. Planning is part of the decision-making process. By planning is meant the development of details of alternative plans of action.
    The key to *effective* planning is

    A. careful research to determine whether a tentative plan has been tried at some time in the past
    B. participation by employees in planning, preferably those employees who will be involved in putting the selected plan into action
    C. speed; poor plans can be discarded after they are put into effect while good plans usually are not put into effect because of delays
    D. writing the plan up in considerable detail and then forwarding the plan, through channels, to the executive officer having final approval of the plan

15. Equating strict discipline with punitive measures and lax discipline with rehabilitation creates a false dichotomy. The one of the statements given below that would BEST follow from the belief expressed in this statement is that discipline

    A. is important for treatment
    B. militates against treatment programs
    C. is not an important consideration in institutions where effective rehabilitation programs prevail
    D. minimizes the need for punitive measures if it is strict

16. If training starts at the lower level of command, it is like planting a seed in tilled ground but removing the sun and rain. Seeds cannot grow unless they have help from above.
    Of the following, the MOST appropriate conclusion to be drawn from this statement is that

    A. the head of an institution may not delegate authority for the planning of an institutional training program for staff
    B. on-the-job training is better than formalized training courses
    C. regularly scheduled training courses must be planned in advance
    D. staff training is the responsibility of higher levels of command

17. The one of the following that BEST describes the meaning of *in-service staff training* is:

    A. The training of personnel who are below average in performance
    B. The training given to each employee throughout his employment
    C. The training of staff only in their own specialized fields
    D. Classroom training where the instructor and employees develop a positive and productive relationship leading to improved efficiency on the job

5 (#1)

18. All bureau personnel should be concerned about, and involved in, public relations. 18.____
    Of the following, the MOST important reason for this statement is that

    A. an institution is an agency of the government supported by public funds and responsible to the public
    B. institutions are places of public business and, therefore, the public is interested in them
    C. some personnel need publicity in order to advance
    D. personnel sometimes need publicity in order to ensure that their grievances are acted upon by higher authority

19. The MOST important factor in establishing a disciplinary policy in an organization is 19.____

    A. consistency of application
    B. strict supervisors
    C. strong enforcement
    D. the degree of toughness or laxity

20. The FIRST step in planning a program is to 20.____

    A. clearly define the objectives
    B. estimate the costs
    C. hire a program director
    D. solicit funds

21. The PRIMARY purpose of control in an organization is to 21.____

    A. punish those who do not do their job well
    B. get people to do what is necessary to achieve an objective
    C. develop clearly stated rules and regulations
    D. regulate expenditures

22. The UNDERLYING principle of *sound* administration is to 22.____

    A. base administration on investigation of facts
    B. have plenty of resources available
    C. hire a strong administrator
    D. establish a broad policy

23. An IMPORTANT aspect to keep in mind during the decision-making process is that 23.____

    A. all possible alternatives for attaining goals should be sought out and considered
    B. considering various alternatives only leads to confusion
    C. once a decision has been made, it cannot be retracted
    D. there is only one correct method to reach any goal

24. Implementation of accountability requires 24.____

    A. a leader who will not hesitate to take punitive action
    B. an established system of communication from the bottom to the top
    C. explicit directives from leaders
    D. too much expense to justify it

25. The CHIEF danger of a decentralized control system is that 25.____
   A. excessive reports and communications will be generated
   B. problem areas may not be detected readily
   C. the expense will become prohibitive
   D. this will result in too many *chiefs*

KEY (CORRECT ANSWERS)

1.	D	11.	D
2.	C	12.	A
3.	B	13.	B
4.	A	14.	B
5.	B	15.	A
6.	A	16.	D
7.	C	17.	B
8.	A	18.	A
9.	A	19.	A
10.	C	20.	A

21.	B
22.	A
23.	A
24.	B
25.	B

TEST 2

DIRECTIONS: Each question or incomplete statement is followed by several suggested answers or completions. Select the one that BEST answers the question or completes the statement. *PRINT THE LETTER OF THE CORRECT ANSWER IN THE SPACE AT THE RIGHT.*

1. When giving orders to his subordinates, a certain supervisor often includes information as to why the work is necessary.
   This approach by the supervisor is *generally*

   A. *inadvisable*, since it appears that he is avoiding responsibility and wishes to blame his superiors
   B. *inadvisable*, since it creates the impression that he is trying to impress the subordinates with his importance
   C. *advisable*, since it serves to motivate the subordinates by giving them a reason for wanting to do the work
   D. *advisable*, since it shows that he is knowledgeable and is in control of his assignments

   1.____

2. Some supervisors often ask capable, professional subordinates to get some work done with questions such as: *Mary, would you try to complete that work today?*
   The use of such request orders *usually*

   A. gets results which are as good as or better than results from direct orders
   B. shows the supervisor to be weak and lowers the respect of his subordinates
   C. provokes resentment as compared to the use of direct orders
   D. leads to confusion as to the proper procedure to follow when carrying out orders

   2.____

3. Assume that a supervisor, because of an emergency when time was essential, and in the absence of his immediate superior, went out of the chain of command to get a decision from a higher level.
   It would consequently be MOST appropriate for the immediate superior to

   A. reprimand him for his action, since the long-range consequences are far more detrimental than the immediate gain
   B. encourage him to use this method, since the chain of command is an outmoded and discredited system which inhibits productive work
   C. order him to refrain from any repetition of this action in the future
   D. support him as long as he informed the superior of the action at the earliest opportunity

   3.____

4. A supervisor gave instructions which he knew were somewhat complex to a subordinate. He then asked the subordinate to repeat the instructions to him.
   The supervisor's decision to have the subordinate repeat the instructions was

   A. *good practice*, mainly because the subordinate would realize the importance of carefully following instructions
   B. *poor practice*, mainly because the supervisor should have given the employee time to ponder the instructions, and then, if necessary, to ask questions
   C. *good practice*, mainly because the supervisor could see whether the subordinate had any apparent problem in understanding the instructions
   D. *poor practice*, mainly because the subordinate should not be expected to have the same degree of knowledge as the supervisor

   4.____

5. Supervisors and subordinates must successfully communicate with each other in order to work well together.
Which of the following statements concerning communication of this type is CORRECT?

   A. When speaking to his subordinates, a supervisor should make every effort to appear knowledgeable about all aspects of their work.
   B. Written communications should be prepared by the supervisor at his own level of comprehension.
   C. The average employee tends to give meaning to communication according to his personal interpretation.
   D. The effective supervisor communicates as much information as he has available to anyone who is interested.

6. A supervisor should be aware of situations in which it is helpful to put his orders to his subordinates in writing.
Which of the following situations would MOST likely call for a WRITTEN order rather than an ORAL order? The order

   A. gives complicated instructions which vary from ordinary practice
   B. involves the performance of duties for which the subordinate is responsible
   C. directs subordinates to perform duties similar to those which they performed in the recent past
   D. concerns a matter that must be promptly completed or dealt with

7. Assume that a supervisor discovers that a false rumor about possible layoffs has spread among his subordinates through the grapevine.
Of the following, the BEST way for the supervisor to deal with this situation is to

   A. use the grapevine to leak accurate information
   B. call a meeting to provide information and to answer questions
   C. post a notice on the bulletin board denying the rumor
   D. institute procedures designed to eliminate the grapevine

8. Communications in an organization with many levels becomes subject to different interpretations at each level and have a tendency to become distorted. The more levels there are in an organization, the greater the likelihood that the final recipient of a communication will get the wrong message.
The one of the following statements which BEST supports the foregoing viewpoint is:

   A. Substantial communications problems exist at high management levels in organizations.
   B. There is a relationship in an organization between the number of hierarchical levels and interference with communications.
   C. An opportunity should be given to subordinates at all levels to communicate their views with impunity.
   D. In larger organizations, there tends to be more interference with downward communications than with upward communications.

9. A subordinate comes to you, his supervisor, to ask a detailed question about a new agency directive; however, you do not know the answer.
Of the following, the MOST helpful response to give the subordinate is to

   A. point out that since your own supervisor has failed to keep you informed of this matter, it is probably unimportant
   B. give the most logical interpretation you can, based on your best judgment
   C. ask him to raise the question with other supervisors until he finds one who knows the answer, then let you know also
   D. explain that you do not know and assure him that you will get the information for him

10. The traditional view of management theory is that communication in an organization should follow the table of organization. A newer theory holds that timely communication often requires bypassing certain steps in the hierarchical chain.
However, the MAIN advantage of using formal channels of communication within an organization is that

   A. an employee is thereby restricted in his relationships to his immediate superior and his immediate subordinates
   B. information is thereby transmitted to everyone who should be informed
   C. the organization will have an appeal channel, or a mechanism by which subordinates can go over their superior's head
   D. employees are thereby encouraged to exercise individual initiative

11. It is unfair to hold subordinates responsible for the performance of duties for which they do not have the requisite authority.
When this is done, it violates the principle that

   A. responsibility *cannot be greater* than that implied by delegated authority
   B. responsibility *should be greater* than that implied by delegated authority
   C. authority *cannot be greater* than that implied by delegated responsibility
   D. authority *should be greater* than that implied by delegated responsibility

12. Assume that a supervisor wishes to delegate some tasks to a capable subordinate.
It would be MOST in keeping with the principles of delegation for the supervisor to

   A. ask another supervisor who is experienced in the delegated tasks to evaluate the subordinate's work from time to time
   B. monitor continually the subordinate's performance by carefully reviewing his work at every step
   C. request experienced employees to submit peer ratings of the work of the subordinate
   D. tell the subordinates what problems are likely to be encountered and specify which problems to report on

13. There are *three* types of leadership: *autocratic,* in which the leader makes the decisions and seeks compliance from his subordinates; *democratic,* in which the leader consults with his subordinates and lets them help set policy; and *free rein,* in which the leader acts as an information center and exercises minimum control over his subordinates.
A supervisor can be MOST effective if he decides to

    A. use democratic leadership techniques exclusively
    B. avoid the use of autocratic leadership techniques entirely
    C. employ the three types of leadership according to the situation
    D. rely mainly on autocratic leadership techniques

14. During a busy period of work, Employee A asked his supervisor for leave in order to take an ordinary vacation. The supervisor denied the request. The following day, Employee B asked for leave during the same period because his wife had just gone to the hospital for an indeterminate stay and he had family matters to tend to.
Of the following, the BEST way for the supervisor to deal with Employee B's request is to

    A. grant the request and give the reason to the other employee
    B. suggest that the employee make his request to higher management
    C. delay the request immediately since granting it would show favoritism
    D. defer any decision until the duration of the hospital stay is determined

15. Assume that you are a supervisor and that a subordinate tells you he has a grievance. In general, you should FIRST

    A. move the grievance forward in order to get a prompt decision
    B. discourage this type of behavior on the part of subordinates
    C. attempt to settle the grievance
    D. refer the subordinate to the personnel office

16. A supervisor may have available a large variety of rewards he can use to motivate his subordinates. However, some supervisors choose the wrong rewards.
A supervisor is *most likely* to make such a mistake if he

    A. appeals to a subordinate's desire to be well regarded by his co-workers
    B. assumes that the subordinate's goals and preferences are the same as his own
    C. conducts in-depth discussions with a subordinate in order to discover his preference
    D. limits incentives to those rewards which he is authorized to provide or to recommend

17. Employee performance appraisal is open to many kinds of errors.
When a supervisor is preparing such an appraisal, he is *most likely* to commit an error if

    A. employees are indifferent to the consequences of their performance appraisals
    B. the entire period for which the evaluation is being made is taken into consideration
    C. standard measurement criteria are used as performance benchmarks
    D. personal characteristics of employees which are not job-related are given weight

18. Assume that a supervisor finds that a report prepared by an employee is unsatisfactory and should be done over. Which of the following should the supervisor do?

    A. Give the report to another employee who can complete it properly.
    B. Have the report done over by the same employee after successfully training him.
    C. Hold a meeting to train all the employees so as not to single out the employee who performed unsatisfactorily
    D. Accept the report so as not to discourage the employee and then make the corrections himself.

19. Employees sometimes wish to have personal advice and counseling, in confidence, about their job-related problems. These problems may include such concerns as health matters, family difficulties, alcoholism, debts, emotional disturbances, etc.
    Such assistance is BEST provided through

    A. maintenance of an exit interview program to find reasons for, and solutions to, turnover problems
    B. arrangements for employees to discuss individual problems informally outside normal administrative channels
    C. procedures which allow employees to submit anonymous inquiries to the personnel department
    D. special hearing committees consisting of top management in addition to immediate supervisors

20. An employee is always a member of some unit of the formal organization. He may also be a member of an informal work group.
    With respect to employee productivity and job satisfaction, the informal work group can MOST accurately be said to

    A. have no influence of any kind on its members
    B. influence its members negatively only
    C. influence its members positively only
    D. influence its members negatively or positively

21. In order to encourage employees to make suggestions, many public agencies have employee suggestion programs.
    What is the MAJOR benefit of such a program to the agency as a whole? It

    A. brings existing or future problems to management's attention
    B. reduces the number of minor accidents
    C. requires employees to share in decision-making responsibilities
    D. reveals employees who have inadequate job knowledge

22. Assume that you have been asked to interview a seemingly shy applicant for a temporary position in your department.
    For you to ask the kinds of questions that begin with *What, Where, Why, When, Who, and How, is*

    A. *good practice*; it informs the applicant that he must conform to the requirements of the department
    B. *poor practice*; it exceeds the extent and purpose of an initial interview
    C. *good practice*; it encourages the applicant to talk to a greater extent
    D. *poor practice*; it encourages the applicant to dominate the discussion

23. In recent years, job enlargement or job enrichment has tended to replace job simplification.
Those who advocate job enrichment or enlargement consider it *desirable* CHIEFLY because

    A. it allows supervisors to control closely the activities of subordinates
    B. it produces greater job satisfaction through reduction of responsibility
    C. most employees prefer to avoid work which is new and challenging
    D. positions with routinized duties are unlikely to provide job satisfaction

24. Job rotation is a training method in which an employee temporarily changes places with another employee of equal rank.
What is usually the MAIN purpose of job rotation? To

    A. politely remove the person being rotated from an unsuitable assignment
    B. increase skills and provide broader experience
    C. prepare the person being rotated for a permanent change
    D. test the skills of the person being rotated

25. There are several principles that a supervisor needs to know if he is to deal adequately with his training responsibilities.
Which of the following is usually NOT a principle of training?

    A. People should be trained according to their individual needs.
    B. People can learn by being told or shown how to do work, but best of all by doing work under guidance.
    C. People can be easily trained even if they have no desire to learn.
    D. Training should be planned, scheduled, executed, and evaluated systematically.

KEY (CORRECT ANSWERS)

1. C
2. A
3. D
4. C
5. C

6. A
7. B
8. B
9. D
10. B

11. A
12. D
13. C
14. A
15. C

16. B
17. D
18. B
19. B
20. D

21. A
22. C
23. D
24. B
25. C

DOCUMENTS AND FORMS
PREPARING WRITTEN MATERIALS

EXAMINATION SECTION
TEST 1

DIRECTIONS: Each question or incomplete statement is followed by several suggested answers or completions. Select the one that BEST answers the question or completes the statement. *PRINT THE LETTER OF THE CORRECT ANSWER IN THE SPACE AT THE RIGHT.*

1. Of the following types of documents, it is MOST important to retain and file

   A. working drafts of reports that have been submitted in final form
   B. copies of letters of good will which conveyed a message that could not be handled by phone
   C. interoffice orders for materials which have been received and verified
   D. interoffice memoranda regarding the routine of standard forms

2. The MAXIMUM number of 2 3/4" x 4 1/4" size forms which may be obtained from one ream of 17" x 22" paper is

   A. 4,000   B. 8,000   C. 12,000   D. 16,000

3. On a general organization chart, staff positions NORMALLY should be pictured

   A. directly above the line positions to which they report
   B. to the sides of the main flow lines
   C. within the box of the highest level subordinate positions pictured
   D. directly below the line positions which report to them

4. When an administrator is diagramming an office layout, of the following, his PRIMARY job *generally* should be to indicate the

   A. lighting intensities that will be required by each operator
   B. noise level that will be produced by the various equipment employed in the office
   C. direction of the work flow and the distance involved in each transfer
   D. durability of major pieces of office equipment currently in use or to be utilized

5. One common guideline or rule-of-thumb ratio for evaluating the efficiency of files is the number of records requested divided by the number of records filed. *Generally,* if this ratio is very low, it would point MOST directly to the need for

   A. improving the indexing and coding systems
   B. improving the charge-out procedures
   C. exploring the need for transferring records from active storage to the archives
   D. exploring the need to encourage employees to keep more records in their private files

6. The GREATEST percentage of money spent on preparing and keeping the usual records in an office *generally* is expended for which one of the following?

   A. Renting space in which to place the record-keeping equipment
   B. Paying salaries of record-preparing and record-keeping personnel
   C. Depreciation of purchased record-preparation and record-keeping machines
   D. Paper and forms upon which to place the records

7. In a certain office, file folders are constantly being removed from the files for use by administrators. At the same time, new material is coming in to be filed in some of these folders.
   Of the following, the BEST way to avoid delays in filing of the new material and to keep track of the removed folders is to

   A. keep a sheet listing all folders removed from the file, who has them, and a follow-update to check on their return; attach to this list new material received for filing
   B. put an "out" slip in the place of any file folder removed, telling what folder is missing, date removed, and who has it; file new material received at front of files
   C. put a temporary "out" folder in place of the one removed, giving title or subject, date removed, and who has it; put into this temporary folder any new material received
   D. keep a list of all folders removed and who has them; forward any new material received for filing while a folder is out to the person who has it

8. Folders labeled "Miscellaneous" should be used in an alphabetic filing system MAINLY to

   A. provide quick access to recent material
   B. avoid setting up individual folders for infrequent correspondence
   C. provide temporary storage for less important documents
   D. temporarily hold papers which will not fit into already crowded individual folders

9. Out-of-date and seldom-used records should be removed periodically from the files because

   A. overall responsibility for records will be transferred to the person in charge of the central storage files
   B. duplicate copies of every record are not needed
   C. valuable filing space will be regained and the time needed to find a current record will be cut down
   D. worthwhile suggestions on improving the filing system will result whenever this is done

10. Of the following, the BEST reason for discarding certain material from office files would be that the

    A. files are crowded
    B. material in the files is old
    C. material duplicates information obtainable from other sources in the files
    D. material is referred to most often by employees in an adjoining office

11. Of the following, the MAIN factor contributing to the expense of maintaining an office procedure manual would be the

    A. infrequent use of the manual
    B. need to revise it regularly
    C. cost of loose-leaf binders
    D. high cost of printing

12. The suggestion that memos or directives which circulate among subordinates be initialed by each employee is a

    A. *poor one,* because, with modern copying machines, it would be possible to supply every subordinate with a copy of each message for his personal use
    B. *good one,* because it relieves the supervisor of blame for the action of subordinates who have read and initialed the messages
    C. *poor one,* because initialing the memo or directive is no guarantee that the subordinate has read the material
    D. *good one,* because it can be used as a record by the supervisor to show that his subordinates have received the message and were responsible for reading it

13. Of the following, the MOST important reason for micro filming office records is to

    A. save storage space needed to keep records
    B. make it easier to get records when needed
    C. speed up the classification of information
    D. shorten the time which records must be kept

14. Your office filing cabinets have become so overcrowded that it is difficult to use the files. Of the following, the *most* desirable step for you to take FIRST to relieve this situation would be to

    A. assign your assistant to spend some time each day re-viewing the material in the files and to give you his recommendations as to what material may be discarded
    B. discard all material which has been in the files more than a given number of years
    C. submit a request for additional filing cabinets in your next budget request
    D. transfer enough material to the central storage room of your agency to give you the amount of additional filing space needed

15. In indexing names of business firms and other organizations, one of the rules to be followed is:

    A. The word "and" is considered an indexing unit.
    B. When a firm name includes the full name of a person who is not well known, the person's first name is considered as the first indexing unit.
    C. Usually, the units in a firm name are indexed in the order in which they are written.
    D. When a firm's name is made up of single letters (such as ABC Corp.), the letters taken together are considered as more than one indexing unit.

16. Assume that your unit processes confidential forms which are submitted by persons seeking financial assistance. An individual comes to your office, gives you his name, and states that he would like to look over a form which he sent in about a week ago because he believes he omitted some important information.
    Of the following, the BEST thing for you to do *first* is to

A. locate the proper form
B. call the individual's home telephone number to verify his identity
C. ask the individual if he has proof of his identity
D. call the security office

17. An employee has been assigned to open her division head's mail and place it on his desk. One day, the employee opens a letter which she then notices is marked "Personal." Of the following, the BEST action for her to take is to

   A. write "Personal" on the letter and staple the envelope to the back of the letter
   B. ignore the matter and treat the letter the same way as the others
   C. give it to another division head to hold until her own division head comes into the office
   D. leave the letter in the envelope and write "Sorry-opened by mistake" on the envelope, and initial it

18. The MOST important reason for having a filing system is to

   A. get papers out of the way
   B. have a record of everything that has happened
   C. retain information to justify your actions
   D. enable rapid retrieval of information

19. The system of filing which is used MOST frequently is called

   A. alphabetic filing   B. alphanumeric filing
   C. geographic filing   D. numeric filing

20. In judging the adequacy of a standard office form, which of the following is LEAST important?

   A. Date of the form   B. Legibility of the form
   C. Size of the form   D. Design of the form

21. Assume that, the letters and reports which are dictated to you fall into a few distinct subject-matter areas.
    The practice of trying to familiarize yourself with the terminology in these areas is

   A. *good,* because you will have a basis for commenting on the dictated material
   B. *good,* because it will be easier to take the dictation at the rate at which it is given
   C. *poor,* because the functions and policies of an office are not of your concern
   D. *poor,* because it will take too much time away from your assigned work

22. A letter was dictated on June 9 and was ready to be typed on June 12. The letter was typed on June 13, signed on June 14, and mailed on June 14. The date that, *ordinarily,* should have appeared on the letter is

   A. June 9   B. June 12
   C. June 13   D. June 14

23. Of the following, the BEST reason for putting the "*key point*" at the beginning of a letter is that it

    A. may save time for the reader
    B. is standard practice in writing letters
    C. will more likely be typed correctly
    D. cannot logically be placed elsewhere

24. As a supervisor, you have been asked to attend committee meetings and take the minutes.
    The body of such minutes, *generally*, consists of

    A. the date and place of the meeting and the list of persons present
    B. an exact verbatim report of everything that was said by each person who spoke
    C. a clear description of each matter discussed and the action decided on
    D. the agenda of the meeting

25. When typing a rough draft from a transcribing machine, a stenographer under your supervision reaches a spot on the tape that is virtually inaudible.
    Of the following, the MOST advisable action that you should recommend to her is to

    A. guess what the dictator intended to say based on what he said in the parts that are clear
    B. ask the dictator to listen to his unsatisfactory dictation
    C. leave an appropriate amount of space for that portion that is inaudible
    D. stop typing the draft and send a note to the dictator identifying the item that could not be completed

KEYS (CORRECT ANSWERS)

1.	D	11.	B
2.	D	12.	D
3.	B	13.	A
4.	C	14.	A
5.	C	15.	C
6.	B	16.	C
7.	C	17.	D
8.	B	18.	D
9.	C	19.	A
10.	C	20.	A

21.	B
22.	D
23.	A
24.	C
25.	C

TEST 2

DIRECTIONS: Each question or incomplete statement is followed by several suggested answers or completions. Select the one that BEST answers the question or completes the statement. *PRINT THE LETTER OF THE CORRECT ANSWER IN THE SPACE AT THE RIGHT.*

1. To tell a newly employed clerk to fill a top drawer of a four-drawer cabinet with heavy folders which will be often used and to keep lower drawers only partly filled, is

    A. *good,* because a tall person would have to bend unnecessarily if he had to use a lower drawer
    B. *bad,* because the file cabinet may tip over when the top drawer is opened
    C. *good,* because it is the most easily reachable drawer for the average person
    D. *bad,* because a person bending down at another drawer may accidentally bang his head on the bottom of the drawer when he straightens up

    1.____

2. If you have requisitioned a "ream" of paper in order to duplicate a single page office announcement, how many announcements can be printed from the one package of paper?

    A. 200   B. 500   C. 700   D. 1,000

    2.____

3. In the operations of a government agency, a voucher is ORDINARILY used to

    A. refer someone to the agency for a position or assignment
    B. certify that an agency's records of financial transactions are accurate
    C. order payment from agency funds of a stated amount to an individual
    D. enter a statement of official opinion in the records of the agency

    3.____

4. Of the following types of cards used in filing systems, the one which is generally MOST helpful in locating records which might be filed under more than one subject is the

    A. out card   B. tickler card
    C. cross-reference card D. visible index card

    4.____

5. The type of filing system in which one does NOT need to refer to a card index in order to find the folder is called

    A. alphabetic   B. geographic
    C. subject   D. locational

    5.____

6. Of the following, records management is LEAST concerned with

    A. the development of the best method for retrieving important information
    B. deciding what records should be kept
    C. deciding the number of appointments a client will need
    D. determining the types of folders to be used

    6.____

7. If records are continually removed from a set of files without "charging" them to the borrower, the filing system will soon become ineffective.
Of the following terms, the one which is NOT applied to a form used in the charge-out system is a

    A. requisition card   B. out-folder
    C. record retrieval form D. substitution card

    7.____

8. A new clerk has been told to put 500 cards in alphabetical order. Another clerk suggests that she divide the cards into four groups such as A to F, G to L, M to R, and S to Z, and then alphabetize these four smaller groups. The suggested method is

   A. *poor*, because the clerk will have to handle the sheets more than once and will waste time
   B. *good* because it saves time, is more accurate, and is less tiring
   C. *good*, because she will not have to concentrate on it so much when it is in smaller groups
   D. *poor*, because this method is much more tiring than straight alphabetizing

9. In Microsoft Excel, data and records are entered into

   A. pages   B. forms   C. cells   D. contracts

10. Suppose a clerk has been given pads of pre-printed forms to use when taking phone messages for others in her office. The clerk is then observed using scraps of paper and not the forms for writing her messages.
    It should be explained that the BEST reason for using the forms is that

    A. they act as a check list to make sure that the important information is taken
    B. she is expected to do her work in the same way as others in the office
    C. they make sure that unassigned paper is not wasted on phone messages
    D. learning to use these forms will help train her to use more difficult forms

11. The high-speed printing process used for producing large quantities of SUPERIOR quality copy and cost efficency is called

    A. photocopying   B. laser printing
    C. inkjet printing   D. word processing

12. Of the following, the MAIN reason a stock clerk keeps a perpetual inventory of supplies in the storeroom is that such an inventory will

    A. eliminate the need for a physical inventory
    B. provide a continuous record of supplies on hand
    C. indicate whether a shipment of supplies is satisfactory
    D. dictate the terms of the purchase order

13. As a supervisor, you may be required to handle different types of correspondence.
    Of the following types of letters, it would be MOST important to promptly seal which kind of letter?

    A. One marked "confidential"
    B. Those containing enclosures
    C. Any letter to be sent airmail
    D. Those in which copies will be sent along with the original

14. While opening incoming mail, you notice that one letter indicates that an enclosure was to be included but, even after careful inspection, you are not able to find the information to which this refers.
    Of the following, the thing that you should do FIRST is

    A. replace the letter in its envelope and return it to the sender
    B. file the letter until the sender's office mails the missing information

C. type out a letter to the sender informing him of his error
D. make a notation in the margin of the letter that the enclosure was omitted

15. You have been given a check list and assigned the responsibility of inspecting certain equipment in the various offices of your agency.
Which of the following is the GREATEST advantage of the check list?

    A. It indicates which equipment is in greatest demand.
    B. Each piece of equipment on the check list will be checked only once.
    C. It helps to insure that the equipment listed will not be overlooked.
    D. The equipment listed suggests other equipment you should look for.

15.____

16. The BEST way to evaluate the overall state of completion of a construction project is to check the progress estimate against the

    A. inspection work sheet
    B. construction schedule
    C. inspector's check list
    D. equipment maintenance schedule

16.____

17. The usual contract for agency work includes a section entitled, "Instructions to Bidders," which states that the

    A. contractor agrees that he has made his own examination and will make no claim for damages on account of errors or omissions
    B. contractor shall not make claims for damages of any discrepancy, error or omission in any plans
    C. estimates of quantities and calculations are guaranteed by the agency to be correct and are deemed to be a representation of the conditions affecting the work
    D. plans, measurements, dimensions and conditions under which the work is to be performed are guaranteed by the agency

17.____

18. In order to avoid disputes over payments for extra work in a contract for construction, the BEST procedure to follow would be to

    A. have contractor submit work progress reports daily
    B. insert a special clause in the contract specifications
    C. have a representative on the job at all times to verify conditions
    D. allocate a certain percentage of the cost of the job to cover such expenses

18.____

19. Prior to the installation of equipment called for in the specifications, the contractor is USUALLY required to submit for approval

    A. sets of shop drawings
    B. a set of revised specifications
    C. a detailed description of the methods of work to be used
    D. a complete list of skilled and unskilled tradesmen he proposes to use

19.____

20. During the actual construction work, the CHIEF value of a construction schedule is to 20.____
    A. insure that the work will be done on time
    B. reveal whether production is falling behind
    C. show how much equipment and material is required for the project
    D. furnish data as to the methods and techniques of construction operations

---

KEYS (CORRECT ANSWERS)

1.	B	11.	B
2.	B	12.	B
3.	C	13.	A
4.	C	14.	D
5.	A	15.	C
6.	C	16.	B
7.	C	17.	A
8.	B	18.	C
9.	C	19.	A
10.	A	20.	B

READING COMPREHENSION
UNDERSTANDING AND INTERPRETING WRITTEN MATERIAL
EXAMINATION SECTION
TEST 1

DIRECTIONS: Each question or incomplete statement is followed by several suggested answers or completions. Select the one that BEST answers the question or completes the statement. *PRINT THE LETTER OF THE CORRECT ANSWER IN THE SPACE AT THE RIGHT.*

Questions 1-3.

DIRECTIONS: Questions 1 through 3 are to be answered SOLELY on the basis of the following paragraph.

The aging housing inventory presents a broad spectrum of conditions, from good upkeep to unbelievable deterioration. Buildings, even relatively good buildings, are likely to have numerous minor violations rather than the gross and evident sanitary violations of an earlier age. Except for the serious violations in a relatively small number of slum buildings, the task is to deal with masses of minor violations that, though insignificant in themselves, amount in the aggregate to major deprivations of health and comfort to tenants. Caused by wear and tear, by the abrasions of time, and aggravated by neglect, these conditions do not readily yield to the dramatic *vacate and restore* measures of earlier times. Moreover, the lines between *good* and *bad* housing have become blurred in many parts of our cities; we find a range of *shades of gray* blending into each other. Different kinds of code enforcement efforts may be required to deal with different degrees of deterioration.

1. The above passage suggests that code enforcement efforts may have to be

    A. developed to cope with varying levels of housing dilapidation
    B. aimed primarily at the serious violations in slum buildings
    C. modeled on the *vacate and restore* measures of earlier times
    D. modified to reduce unrealistic penalties for petty violations

2. According to the above passage, during former times some buildings had sanitary violations which were

    A. irreparable and minor
    B. blurred and gray
    C. flagrant and obvious
    D. insignificant and numerous

3. According to the above passage, the aging housing stock presents a

    A. great number of rent-controlled buildings
    B. serious problem of tenant-caused deterioration
    C. significant increase in buildings without intentional violations
    D. wide range of physical conditions

Questions 4-5.

DIRECTIONS: Questions 4 and 5 are to be answered SOLELY on the basis of the following passage.

    In general, housing code provisions relating to the safe and sanitary maintenance of dwelling units prescribe the maintenance required for foundations, walls, ceilings, floors, windows, doors, stairways, and also the facilities and equipment required in other sections. The more recent codes have, in addition, extensive provisions designed to ensure that the unit be maintained in a rat-free and rat-proof condition. Also, as an example of new approaches in code provisions, one proposed Federal model housing code prohibits the landlord from terminating vital services and utilities except during temporary emergencies or when actual repairs or maintenance are in process. This provision may be used to prevent a landlord from turning off utility services as a technique of self-help eviction or as a weapon against rent strikes.

4. According to the above passage, the more recent housing codes have extensive provisions designed to 4.____

    A. maintain a reasonably fire-proof living unit
    B. prohibit tenants from participating in rent strikes
    C. maintain the unit free from rats
    D. prohibit tenants from using lead-based paints

5. According to the above passage, one housing code would permit landlords to terminate vital services during 5.____

    A. a rent strike
    B. an actual eviction
    C. a temporary emergency
    D. the planning of repairs and maintenance

Questions 6-8.

DIRECTIONS: Questions 6 through 8 are to be answered SOLELY on the basis of the following passage.

    City governments have long had building codes which set minimum standards for building and for human occupancy. The code (or series of codes) makes provisions for standards of lighting and ventilation, sanitation, fire prevention, and protection. As a result of demands from manufacturers, builders, real estate people, tenement owners, and building-trades unions, these codes often have established minimum standards well below those that the contemporary society would accept as a rock-bottom minimum. Codes often become outdated so that meager standards in one era become seriously inadequate a few decades later as society"s concept of a minimum standard of living changes. Out-of-date codes, when still in use, have sometimes prevented the introduction of new devices and modern building techniques. Thus, it is extremely important that building codes keep pace with changes in the accepted concept of a minimum standard of living.

6. According to the above passage, all of the following considerations in building planning would probably be covered in a building code EXCEPT

   A. closet space as a percentage of total floor area
   B. size and number of windows required for rooms of differing sizes
   C. placement of fire escapes in each line of apartments
   D. type of garbage disposal units to be installed

7. According to the above passage, if an ideal building code were to be created, how would the established minimum standards in it compare to the ones that are presently set by city governments?
   They would

   A. be lower than they are at present
   B. be higher than they are at present
   C. be comparable to the present minimum standards
   D. vary according to the economic group that sets them

8. On the basis of the above passage, what is the reason for difficulties in introducing new building techniques?

   A. Builders prefer techniques which represent the rock-bottom minimum desired by society.
   B. Certain manufacturers have obtained patents on various building methods to the exclusion of new techniques.
   C. The government does not want to invest money in techniques that will soon be outdated.
   D. New techniques are not provided for in building codes which are not up-to-date.

Questions 9-11.

DIRECTIONS: Questions 9 through 11 are to be answered SOLELY on the basis of the following paragraph.

When constructed within a multiple dwelling, such storage space shall be equipped with a sprinkler system and also with a system of mechanical ventilation in no way connected with any other ventilating system. Such storage space shall have no opening into any other part of the dwelling except through a fireproof vestibule. Any such vestibule shall have a minimum superficial floor area of fifty square feet, and its maximum area shall not exceed seventy-five square feet. It shall be enclosed with incombustible partitions having a fire-resistive rating of three hours. The floor and ceiling of such vestibule shall also be of incombustible material having a fire-resistive rating of at least three hours. There shall be two doors to provide access from the dwelling, to the car storage space. Each such door shall have a fire-resistive rating of one and one-half hours and shall be provided with a device to prevent the opening of one door until the other door is entirely closed.

9. According to the above paragraph, the one of the following that is REQUIRED in order for cars to be permitted to be stored in a multiple dwelling is a(n)

   A. fireproof vestibule
   B. elevator from the garage
   C. approved heating system
   D. sprinkler system

10. According to the above paragraph, the one of the following materials that would NOT be acceptable for the walls of a vestibule connecting a garage to the dwelling portion of a building is

   A. 3" solid gypsum blocks
   B. 4" brick
   C. 4" hollow gypsum blocks, plastered both sides
   D. 6" solid cinder concrete blocks

11. According to the above paragraph, the one of the following that would be ACCEPTABLE for the width and length of a vestibule connecting a garage that is within a multiple dwelling to the dwelling portion of the building is

   A. 3'8" x 13'0"   B. 4'6" x 18'6"
   C. 4'9" x 14'6"   D. 4'3" x 19'3"

Questions 12-13.

DIRECTIONS: Questions 12 and 13 are to be answered SOLELY on the basis of the following paragraph.

It shall be unlawful to place, use, or maintain in a condition intended, arranged, or designed for use, any gas-fired cooking appliance, laundry stove, heating stove, range or water heater or combination of such appliances in any room or space used for living or sleeping in any new or existing multiple dwelling unless such room or space has a window opening to the outer air or such gas appliance is vented to the outer air. All automatically operated gas appliances shall be equipped with a device which shall shut off automatically the gas supply to the main burners when the pilot light in such appliance is extinguished. A gas range or the cooking portion of a gas appliance incorporating a room heater shall not be deemed an automatically operated gas appliance. However, burners in gas ovens and broilers which can be turned on and off or ignited by non-manual means shall be equipped with a device which shall shut off automatically the gas supply to those burners when the operation of such non-manual means fails.

12. According to the above paragraph, an automatic shut-off device is NOT required on a gas

   A. hot water heater   B. laundry dryer
   C. space heater   D. range

13. According to the above paragraph, a gas-fired water heater is permitted

   A. only in kitchens   B. only in bathrooms
   C. only in living rooms   D. in any type of room

Questions 14-18.

DIRECTIONS: Questions 14 through 18 are to be answered SOLELY on the basis of the information contained in the statement below.

No multiple dwelling shall be erected to a height in excess of one and one-half times the width of the widest street on which it faces, except that above the level of such height, for each one foot that the front wall of such dwelling sets back from the street line, three feet shall be added to the height limit of such dwelling, but such dwelling shall not exceed in maximum height three feet plus one and three-quarter times the width of the widest street on which it faces.

Any such dwelling facing a street more than one hundred feet in width shall be subject to the same height limitations as though such dwelling faced a street one hundred feet in width.

14. The MAXIMUM height of a multiple dwelling set back five feet from the street line and facing a 60 foot wide street is ____ feet.

    A. 60   B. 90   C. 105   D. 165

15. The MAXIMUM height of a multiple dwelling set back six feet from the street line and facing a 120 foot wide street is ____ feet.

    A. 198   B. 168   C. 120   D. 105

16. The MAXIMUM height of a multiple dwelling is

    A. 100 ft.   B. 150 ft.   C. 178 ft.   D. unlimited

17. The MAXIMUM height of a multiple dwelling set back 10 feet from the street line and facing a 110 foot wide street is ____ feet.

    A. 178   B. 180   C. 195   D. 205

18. The MAXIMUM height of a multiple dwelling set back eight feet from the street line and facing a 90 foot wide street is ____ feet.

    A. 135   B. 147   C. 178   D. 159

Questions 19-23.

DIRECTIONS: Questions 19 through 23 are to be answered SOLELY on the basis of the following statement.

The number of persons accommodated on any story in a lodging house shall not be greater than the sum of the following components,

   a. 22 persons for each full multiple of 22 inches in the smallest clear width for each means of egress approved by the department, other than fire escapes
   b. 20 persons for each lawful fire escape accessible from such story.

19. The MAXIMUM number of persons that may be accommodated on a story in a lodging house depends on the

    A. number of lawful fire escapes *only*
    B. number of approved means of egress *only*
    C. smallest clear width in each approved means of egress *only*
    D. number of lawful fire escapes and sum total of smallest clear widths in each approved means of egress

20. The MAXIMUM number of persons that may be accommodated on a story of a lodging house having one lawful fire escape and a sum total of 44 inches in the smallest clear widths of the two approved means of egress is

    A. 20   B. 22   C. 42   D. 64

21. The MAXIMUM number of persons that may be accommodated on a story of a lodging house having two lawful fire escapes and a sum total of 60 inches in the smallest clear width of the approved means of egress is

   A. 64   B. 84   C. 100   D. 106

22. The MAXIMUM number of persons that may be accommodated on a story of a lodging house having one lawful fire escape and a sum total of 33 inches in the smallest clear width of the approved means of egress is

   A. 42   B. 53   C. 64   D. 73

23. The MAXIMUM number of persons that may be accommodated on a story of a lodging house having two lawful fire escapes and two approved means of egress, with 40 inches and 44 inches in the smallest clear widths, respectively, is

   A. 84   B. 104   C. 106   D. 108

Questions 24-25.

DIRECTIONS: Questions 24 and 25 are to be answered SOLELY on the basis of the following paragraph.

Though the recent trend toward apartment construction may appear to be the Region's response to large-lot zoning and centralized industry, it really is not. It is mainly a function of the age of the population. Most of the apartments are occupied by one- and two-person families young people out of school but without a family of their own and older people whose children have grown. Both groups have been increasing in number; and, in this Region, they characteristically live in apartments. It is this increased demand for apartments and the simultaneous decrease in demand for one-family houses that dramatically raised the percentage of building permits issued for multi-family housing units from 36 percent in 1977 to 67 percent in 1981. The fact that three-fourths of the apartments were built in the Core between 1977 and 1981 at the same time as the Core was losing population underscores the failure of the apartment boom to slow the outward spread of the population.

24. According to the above paragraph, one of the reasons for the increase in the number of building permits issued for multi-family construction in the City Metropolitan Region is

   A. that workers in industry want to live close to their jobs
   B. an increase in the number of elderly people living in the Region
   C. the inability of many families to afford the large lots necessary to build private homes
   D. the new zoning ordinance made it easier to build apartments

25. According to the above paragraph, the apartment construction boom

   A. increased the population density in the Core
   B. spurred a population shift to the suburbs
   C. did not halt the outward flow of the population from the Core
   D. was most significant in the outer areas of the Region

KEY (CORRECT ANSWERS)

1. A
2. C
3. D
4. C
5. C

6. A
7. B
8. D
9. D
10. B

11. C
12. D
13. D
14. C
15. B

16. C
17. A
18. D
19. D
20. D

21. B
22. A
23. C
24. B
25. C

TEST 2

DIRECTIONS: Each question or incomplete statement is followed by several suggested answers or completions. Select the one that BEST answers the question or completes the statement. *PRINT THE LETTER OF THE CORRECT ANSWER IN THE SPACE AT THE RIGHT.*

Questions 1-4.

DIRECTIONS: Questions 1 through 4 are to be answered SOLELY on the basis of the following paragraph.

Although the suburbs have provided housing and employment for millions of additional families since 1950, many suburban communities have maintained controls over the kinds of families who can live in them. Suburban attitudes have been formed by reaction against a perception of crowded, harassed city life and threatening alien city people. As population, taxable income, and jobs have left the cities for the suburbs, the *urban crisis* of substandard housing, declining levels of education and public services, and decreasing employment opportunities has been created. The crisis, however, is not urban at all, but national, and in part a result of the suburban policy that discourages outward movement by the urban poor.

1. According to the above paragraph, the quality of urban life   1.____

    A. is determined by public opinion in the cities
    B. has worsened in recent years
    C. is similar to rural life
    D. can be changed by political means

2. According to the above paragraph, suburban communities have   2.____

    A. tried to show that the urban crisis is really a national crisis
    B. avoided taking a position on the urban crisis
    C. been involved in causing the urban crisis
    D. been the innocent victims of the urban crisis

3. According to the above paragraph, the poor have   3.____

    A. become increasingly sophisticated in their attempts to move to the suburbs
    B. generally been excluded from the suburbs
    C. lost incentive for betterment of their living conditions
    D. sought improvement of the central cities

4. As used in the above paragraph, the word perception means MOST NEARLY   4.____

    A. development   B. impression
    C. opposition   D. uncertainty

Questions 5-8.

DIRECTIONS: Questions 5 through 8 are to be answered SOLELY on the basis of the following paragraph.

The concentration of publicly assisted housing in central cities -- because the suburbs do not want them and effectively bar them -- is usually rationalized by a solicitous regard for keeping intact the city neighborhoods cherished by low-income groups. If one accepted this as valid, the devotion of minorities to blighted city neighborhoods in preference to suburban employment and housing would be an historic first. Certainly no such devotion was visible among the millions who have deserted their city neighborhoods in the last 25 years even if it meant an arduous daily trip from the suburbs to their jobs in the cities.

5. The writer implies that MOST poor people

   A. prefer isolation
   B. fear change
   C. are angry
   D. seek betterment

6. The general tone of the paragraph is BEST characterized as

   A. uncertain   B. skeptical   C. evasive   D. indifferent

7. As used in the above paragraph, the word <u>rationalize</u> means MOST NEARLY

   A. dispute   B. justify   C. deny   D. locate

8. According to the above paragraph, publicly assisted housing is concentrated in the central cities PRIMARILY because

   A. city dwellers are unable to find satisfactory housing
   B. deterioration of older housing has increased in recent years
   C. suburbanites have opposed the movement of the poor to the suburbs
   D. employment opportunities have decreased in the suburbs

Questions 9-11.

DIRECTIONS: Questions 9 through 11 are to be answered SOLELY on the basis of the following paragraph.

In recent years, new and important emphasis has been placed upon the maximum use of conservation and rehabilitation techniques in carrying out programs of urban renewal and revitalization. In urban renewal projects where existing structures are hopelessly deteriorated or land uses are incompatible with the community's overall plans, the entire area may be acquired, cleared, and sold for redevelopment. However, where existing structures are basically sound but have deteriorated to the point where they are a <u>blighting</u> influence on the neighborhood, they may be salvaged through a program of rehabilitation and reconditioning.

9. According to the above paragraph, the one of the following which is MOST likely to cause area-wide razing of the buildings in urban renewal programs is

   A. a program of rehabilitation and reconditioning
   B. concerted insistence by landlords and tenants that certain buildings be bulldozed
   C. an inability of community groups to agree on priorities for staged clearance
   D. land use contrary to the community's general plan

10. According to the above paragraph, rehabilitation of structures may take place if

    A. new conservation and rehabilitation techniques are used
    B. salvaging all the buildings in the entire area is hopeless
    C. the community wishes to preserve historic structures
    D. the existing buildings are structurally sound

11. As used in the above paragraph, the word blighting means MOST NEARLY 11.____

   A. ruining   B. infrequent   C. recurrent   D. traditional

Questions 12-13.

DIRECTIONS: Questions 12 and 13 are to be answered SOLELY on the basis of the following paragraphs.

We must also find better ways to handle the relocation of people uprooted by projects. In the past, many renewal plans have foundered on this problem, and it is still the most difficult part of the community development. Large-scale replacement of low-income residents -- many ineligible for public housing -- has contributed to deterioration of surrounding communities. However, thanks to changes in housing authority procedures, relocation has been accomplished in a far more satisfactory fashion. The step-by-step community development projects we advocate in this plan should bring further improvement.

But additional measures will be necessary. There are going to be more people to be moved; and, with the current shortage of apartments, large ones especially, it is going to be tougher to find places to move them to. The city should have more freedom to buy or lease housing that comes on the market because of normal turnover and make it available to relocatees.

12. According to the above paragraphs, one of the reasons a neighborhood may deteriorate is that 12.____

   A. there is a scarcity of large apartments
   B. step-by-step community development projects have failed
   C. people in the given neighborhood are uprooted from their homes
   D. a nearby renewal project has an inadequate relocation plan

13. From the above paragraphs, one might conclude that the relocation phase of community renewal has been improved. 13.____

   A. by changes in housing authority procedures
   B. by development of step-by-step community development projects
   C. through expanded city powers to buy housing for relocation
   D. by the addition of huge sums of money

Questions 14-15.

DIRECTIONS: Questions 14 and 15 are to be answered SOLELY on the basis of the following paragraphs.

Provision of decent housing for the lower half of the population (by income) was thus taken on as a public responsibility. Public housing was to assist the poorest quarter of urban families while the 221(d)(3) Housing Program would assist the next quarter. But limited funds meant that the supply of subsidized housing could not stretch nearly far enough to help this half of the population. Who were to be left out in the rationing process which was accomplished by the sifting of applicants for housing on the part of public and private authorities?

Discrimination on the grounds of race or color is not allowed under Federal law. In all sections of the country, encouragingly, housing programs are found which follow this law to the letter. Yet, housing programs in some cities still suffer from the residue of racial segregation policies and attitudes that for years were condoned or even encouraged.

Some sifting in the 221(d)(3) Housing Program follows the practice of many public housing authorities, the imposition of requirements with respect to character. This is a delicate matter. To fill a project overwhelmingly with broken families, alcoholics, criminals, delinquents, and other problem tenants would hardly make it a wholesome environment. Yet the total exclusion of such families is hardly an acceptable alternative. To the extent this exclusion is practiced, the very people whose lives are described in order to persuade lawmakers and the public to instigate new programs find the door shut in their faces when such programs come into being. The proper balance is difficult to achieve, but society's neediest families surely should not be totally denied the opportunities for rejuvenation in subsidized housing.

14. From the above paragraphs, it can be assumed that the 221(d)(3) Housing Program

    A. served a population earning more than the median income
    B. served a less affluent population than is served by public housing
    C. excludes all problem families from its projects
    D. is a subsidized housing program

15. According to this text, the provision of housing for the poor

    A. has not been completely accomplished with public monies
    B. is never influenced by segregationist policies
    C. is limited to providing housing for only the neediest families
    D. is primarily the responsibility of the Federal government

16. Five hundred persons attended a public hearing at which a proposed public housing project was being considered. Less than half favored the project while the majority opposed the project.
    According to the above statement, it is REASONABLE to conclude that

    A. the proposal stimulated considerable community interest
    B. the public housing project was disapproved by the city because a majority opposed it
    C. those who opposed the project lacked sympathy for needy persons
    D. the supporters of the project were led by militants

17. A vacant lot close to a polluted creek is for sale. Two buyers compete. One owns an adjacent factory which provides 300 high paying unskilled jobs. He needs to expand or move from the city. If he expands, he will provide 300 additional jobs. The other is a community group in a changing residential area close by. They hope to stabilize the neighborhood by bringing in new housing. They would build an apartment building with 100 dwelling units on the lot.
    According to the above paragraph, it is REASONABLE to conclude that

    A. jobs are more important than housing
    B. there is conflict between the factory owners and the neighborhood group
    C. the neighborhood group will not succeed in stabilizing the area by constructing new housing
    D. the polluted creek should be cleaned up

18. The housing authority faces every problem of the private developer, and it must also assume responsibilities of which private building is free. The authority must account to the community; it must conform to federal regulations; it must provide durable buildings of good standard at low cost; it must overcome the prejudices against public operations, of contractors, bankers, and prospective tenants. These authorities are being watched by anti-housing enthusiasts for the first error of judgment or the first evidence of high costs, to be torn to bits before a Congressional committee.
On the basis of this statement, it would be MOST correct to state that

   A. private builders do not have the opposition of contractors, bankers, and prospective tenants
   B. Congressional committees impede the progress of public housing by petty investigations
   C. a housing authority must deal with all the difficulties encountered by the private builder
   D. housing authorities are no more immune from errors in judgment than private developers

18.____

19. Another factor that has considerably added to the city's housing crisis has been the great influx of low-income workers and their families seeking better employment opportunities during wartime and defense boom periods. The circumstances of these families have forced them to crowd into the worst kind of housing and have produced on a renewed scale the conditions from which slums flourish and grow.
On the basis of this statement, one would be justified in stating that

   A. the influx of low-income workers has aggravated the slum problem
   B. the city has better employment opportunities than other sections of the country
   C. the high wages paid by our defense industries have made many families ineligible for tenancy in public housing projects
   D. the families who settled in the city during wartime and the defense build-up brought with them language and social customs conducive to the growth of slums

19.____

20. Much of the city felt the effects of the general postwar increase of vandalism and street crime, and the greatly expanded public housing program was no exception. Projects built in congested slum areas with a high incidence of delinquency and crime were particularly subjected to the depredations of neighborhood gangs. The civil service watchmen who patrolled the projects, unarmed and neither trained nor expected to perform police duties, were unable to cope with the situation.
On the basis of this statement, the MOST accurate of the following statements is:

   A. Neighborhood gangs were particularly responsible for the high incidence of delinquency and crime in congested slum areas having public housing programs
   B. Civil service watchmen who patrolled housing projects failed to carry out their assigned police duties
   C. Housing projects were not spared the effects of the general postwar increase of vandalism and street crime
   D. Delinquency and crime affected housing projects in slum areas to a greater extent than other dwellings in the same area

20.____

21. Another peculiar characteristic of real estate is the absence of liquidity. Each parcel is a discrete unit as to size, location, rental, physical condition, and financing arrangements. Each property requires investigation, comparison of rents with other properties, and individualized haggling on price and terms.
On the basis of this statement, the LEAST accurate of the following statements is:

    A. Although the size, location, and rent of parcels vary, comparison with rents of other properties affords an indication of the value of a particular parcel
    B. Bargaining skill is the essential factor in determining the value of a parcel of real estate
    C. Each parcel of real estate has individual peculiarities distinguishing it from any other parcel
    D. Real estate is not easily converted to other types of assets

22. In part, at least, the charges of sameness, monotony, and institutionalism directed at public housing projects result from the degree in which they differ from the city's normal housing pattern. They seem alike because their very difference from the usual makes them stand apart.
In many respects, there is considerably more variety between public housing projects than there is between different streets of apartment houses or tenements throughout the city.
On the basis of this statement, it would be LEAST accurate to state that:

    A. There is considerably more variety between public housing projects than there is between different streets of tenements throughout the city
    B. Public housing projects differ from the city's normal housing pattern to the degree that sameness, monotony, and institutionalism are characteristic of public buildings
    C. Public housing projects seem alike because their deviation from the usual dwellings draws attention to them
    D. The variety in structure between public housing projects and other public buildings is related to the period in which they were built

23. The amount of debt that can be charged against the city for public housing is limited by law. Part of the city's restricted housing means goes for cash subsidies it may be required to contribute to state-aided projects. Under the provisions of the state law, the city must match the state's contributions in subsidies; and while the value of the partial tax exemption granted by the city is counted for this purpose, it is not always sufficient.
On the basis of this statement, it would be MOST accurate to state that:

    A. The amount of money the city may spend for public housing is limited by annual tax revenues
    B. The value of tax exemptions granted by the city to educational, religious, and charitable institutions may be added to its subsidy contributions to public housing projects
    C. The subsidy contributions for state-aided public housing projects are shared equally by the state and the city under the provisions of the state law
    D. The tax revenues of the city, unless supplemented by state aid, are insufficient to finance public housing projects

24. Maintenance costs can be minimized and the useful life of houses can be extended by building with the best and most permanent materials available. The best and most permanent materials in many cases are, however, much more expensive than materials which require more maintenance. The most economical procedure in home building has been to compromise between the capital costs of high quality and enduring materials and the maintenance costs of less desirable materials.
On the basis of this statement, one would be justified in stating that:

   A. Savings in maintenance costs make the use of less durable and less expensive building materials preferable to high quality materials that would prolong the useful life of houses constructed from them
   B. Financial advantage can be secured by the home builder if he judiciously combines costly but enduring building materials with less desirable materials which, however, require more maintenance
   C. A compromise between the capital costs of high quality materials and the maintenance costs of less desirable materials makes it easier for a home builder to estimate construction expenditures
   D. The most economical procedure in home building is to balance the capital costs of the most permanent materials against the costs of less expensive materials that are cheaper to maintain

25. Personnel selection has been a critical problem for local housing authorities. The pool of qualified workers trained in housing procedures is small, and the colleges and universities have failed to grasp the opportunity for enlarging it. While real estate experience makes a good background for management of a housing project, many real estate men are deplorably lacking in understanding of social and governmental problems. Social workers, on the other hand, are likely to be deficient in business judgment.
On the basis of this statement, it would be MOST accurate to state that:

   A. Colleges and universities have failed to train qualified workers for proficiency in housing procedures
   B. Social workers are deficient in business judgment as related to the management of a housing project
   C. Real estate experience makes a person a good manager of a housing project
   D. Local housing authorities have been critical of present methods of personnel selection

KEY (CORRECT ANSWERS)

1.	B	11.	A
2.	C	12.	D
3.	B	13.	A
4.	B	14.	D
5.	D	15.	A
6.	B	16.	A
7.	B	17.	B
8.	D	18.	C
9.	D	19.	A
10.	D	20.	C

21. B
22. B
23. C
24. B
25. A

PHILOSOPHY, PRINCIPLES, PRACTICES AND TECHNICS OF SUPERVISION, ADMINISTRATION, MANAGEMENT AND ORGANIZATION

TABLE OF CONTENTS

		Page
I.	MEANING OF SUPERVISION	1
II.	THE OLD AND THE NEW SUPERVISION	1
III.	THE EIGHT (8) BASIC PRINCIPLES OF THE NEW SUPERVISION	1
	1. Principle of Responsibility	1
	2. Principle of Authority	2
	3. Principle of Self-Growth	2
	4. Principle of Individual Worth	2
	5. Principle of Creative Leadership	2
	6. Principle of Success and Failure	2
	7. Principle of Science	3
	8. Principle of Cooperation	3
IV.	WHAT IS ADMINISTRATION?	3
	1. Practices commonly classed as "Supervisory"	3
	2. Practices commonly classed as "Administrative"	3
	3. Practices classified as both "Supervisory" and "Administrative"	4
V.	RESPONSIBILITIES OF THE SUPERVISOR	4
VI.	COMPETENCIES OF THE SUPERVISOR	4
VII.	THE PROFESSIONAL SUPERVISOR—EMPLOYEE RELATIONSHIP	4
VIII.	MINI-TEXT IN SUPERVISION, ADMINISTRATION, MANAGEMENT AND ORGANIZATION	5
	A. Brief Highlights	5
	1. Levels of Management	5
	2. What the Supervisor Must Learn	6
	3. A Definition of Supervision	6
	4. Elements of the Team Concept	6
	5. Principles of Organization	6
	6. The Four Important Parts of Every Job	6
	7. Principles of Delegation	6
	8. Principles of Effective Communications	7
	9. Principles of Work Improvement	7

TABLE OF CONTENTS (CONTINUED)

10. Areas of Job Improvement	7
11. Seven Key Points in Making Improvements	7
12. Corrective Techniques for Job Improvement	7
13. A Planning Checklist	8
14. Five Characteristics of Good Directions	8
15. Types of Directions	8
16. Controls	8
17. Orienting the New Employee	8
18. Checklist for Orienting New Employees	8
19. Principles of Learning	9
20. Causes of Poor Performance	9
21. Four Major Steps in On-The-Job Instructions	9
22. Employees Want Five Things	9
23. Some Don'ts in Regard to Praise	9
24. How to Gain Your Workers' Confidence	9
25. Sources of Employee Problems	9
26. The Supervisor's Key to Discipline	10
27. Five Important Processes of Management	10
28. When the Supervisor Fails to Plan	10
29. Fourteen General Principles of Management	10
30. Change	10

B. Brief Topical Summaries — 11
- I. Who/What is the Supervisor? — 11
- II. The Sociology of Work — 11
- III. Principles and Practices of Supervision — 12
- IV. Dynamic Leadership — 12
- V. Processes for Solving Problems — 12
- VI. Training for Results — 13
- VII. Health, Safety and Accident Prevention — 13
- VIII. Equal Employment Opportunity — 13
- IX. Improving Communications — 14
- X. Self-Development — 14
- XI. Teaching and Training — 14
  - A. The Teaching Process — 14
    1. Preparation — 14
    2. Presentation — 15
    3. Summary — 15
    4. Application — 15
    5. Evaluation — 15
  - B. Teaching Methods — 15
    1. Lecture — 15
    2. Discussion — 15
    3. Demonstration — 16
    4. Performance — 16
    5. Which Method to Use — 16

PHILOSOPHY, PRINCIPLES, PRACTICES, AND TECHNICS
OF
SUPERVISION, ADMINISTRATION, MANAGEMENT AND ORGANIZATION

I. MEANING OF SUPERVISION

The extension of the democratic philosophy has been accompanied by an extension in the scope of supervision. Modern leaders and supervisors no longer think of supervision in the narrow sense of being confined chiefly to visiting employees, supplying materials, or rating the staff. They regard supervision as being intimately related to all the concerned agencies of society, they speak of the supervisor's function in terms of "growth", rather than the "improvement," of employees.

This modern concept of supervision may be defined as follows:

Supervision is leadership and the development of leadership within groups which are cooperatively engaged in inspection, research, training, guidance and evaluation.

II. THE OLD AND THE NEW SUPERVISION

TRADITIONAL
1. Inspection
2. Focused on the employee
3. Visitation
4. Random and haphazard
5. Imposed and authoritarian
6. One person usually

MODERN
1. Study and analysis
2. Focused on aims, materials, methods, supervisors, employees, environment
3. Demonstrations, intervisitation, workshops, directed reading, bulletins, etc.
4. Definitely organized and planned (scientific)
5. Cooperative and democratic
6. Many persons involved (creative)

III THE EIGHT (8) BASIC PRINCIPLES OF THE NEW SUPERVISION

1. *PRINCIPLE OF RESPONSIBILITY*
Authority to act and responsibility for acting must be joined.
   a. If you give responsibility, give authority.
   b. Define employee duties clearly.
   c. Protect employees from criticism by others.
   d. Recognize the rights as well as obligations of employees.
   e. Achieve the aims of a democratic society insofar as it is possible within the area of your work.
   f. Establish a situation favorable to training and learning.
   g. Accept ultimate responsibility for everything done in your section, unit, office, division, department.
   h. Good administration and good supervision are inseparable.

2. PRINCIPLE OF AUTHORITY

The success of the supervisor is measured by the extent to which the power of authority is not used.
- a. Exercise simplicity and informality in supervision.
- b. Use the simplest machinery of supervision.
- c. If it is good for the organization as a whole, it is probably justified.
- d. Seldom be arbitrary or authoritative.
- e. Do not base your work on the power of position or of personality.
- f. Permit and encourage the free expression of opinions.

3. PRINCIPLE OF SELF-GROWTH

The success of the supervisor is measured by the extent to which, and the speed with which, he is no longer needed.
- a. Base criticism on principles, not on specifics.
- b. Point out higher activities to employees.
- c. Train for self-thinking by employees, to meet new situations.
- d. Stimulate initiative, self-reliance and individual responsibility.
- e. Concentrate on stimulating the growth of employees rather than on removing defects.

4. PRINCIPLE OF INDIVIDUAL WORTH

Respect for the individual is a paramount consideration in supervision.
- a. Be human and sympathetic in dealing with employees.
- b. Don't nag about things to be done.
- c. Recognize the individual differences among employees and seek opportunities to permit best expression of each personality.

5. PRINCIPLE OF CREATIVE LEADERSHIP

The best supervision is that which is not apparent to the employee.
- a. Stimulate, don't drive employees to creative action.
- b. Emphasize doing good things.
- c. Encourage employees to do what they do best.
- d. Do not be too greatly concerned with details of subject or method.
- e. Do not be concerned exclusively with immediate problems and activities.
- f. Reveal higher activities and make them both desired and maximally possible.
- g. Determine procedures in the light of each situation but see that these are derived from a sound basic philosophy.
- h. Aid, inspire and lead so as to liberate the creative spirit latent in all good employees.

6. PRINCIPLE OF SUCCESS AND FAILURE

There are no unsuccessful employees, only unsuccessful supervisors who have failed to give proper leadership.
- a. Adapt suggestions to the capacities, attitudes, and prejudices of employees.
- b. Be gradual, be progressive, be persistent.
- c. Help the employee find the general principle; have the employee apply his own problem to the general principle.
- d. Give adequate appreciation for good work and honest effort.
- e. Anticipate employee difficulties and help to prevent them.
- f. Encourage employees to do the desirable things they will do anyway.
- g. Judge your supervision by the results it secures.

7. PRINCIPLE OF SCIENCE
Successful supervision is scientific, objective, and experimental. It is based on facts, not on prejudices.
- a. Be cumulative in results.
- b. Never divorce your suggestions from the goals of training.
- c. Don't be impatient of results.
- d. Keep all matters on a professional, not a personal level.
- e. Do not be concerned exclusively with immediate problems and activities.
- f. Use objective means of determining achievement and rating where possible.

8. PRINCIPLE OF COOPERATION
Supervision is a cooperative enterprise between supervisor and employee.
- a. Begin with conditions as they are.
- b. Ask opinions of all involved when formulating policies.
- c. Organization is as good as its weakest link.
- d. Let employees help to determine policies and department programs.
- e. Be approachable and accessible - physically and mentally.
- f. Develop pleasant social relationships.

IV. WHAT IS ADMINISTRATION?

Administration is concerned with providing the environment, the material facilities, and the operational procedures that will promote the maximum growth and development of supervisors and employees. (Organization is an aspect, and a concomitant, of administration.)

There is no sharp line of demarcation between supervision and administration; these functions are intimately interrelated and, often, overlapping. They are complementary activities.

1. PRACTICES COMMONLY CLASSED AS "SUPERVISORY"
- a. Conducting employees conferences
- b. Visiting sections, units, offices, divisions, departments
- c. Arranging for demonstrations
- d. Examining plans
- e. Suggesting professional reading
- f. Interpreting bulletins
- g. Recommending in-service training courses
- h. Encouraging experimentation
- i. Appraising employee morale
- j. Providing for intervisitation

2. PRACTICES COMMONLY CLASSIFIED AS "ADMINISTRATIVE"
- a. Management of the office
- b. Arrangement of schedules for extra duties
- c. Assignment of rooms or areas
- d. Distribution of supplies
- e. Keeping records and reports
- f. Care of audio-visual materials
- g. Keeping inventory records
- h. Checking record cards and books
- i. Programming special activities
- j. Checking on the attendance and punctuality of employees

3. *PRACTICES COMMONLY CLASSIFIED AS BOTH "SUPERVISORY" AND "ADMINISTRATIVE"*
   a. Program construction
   b. Testing or evaluating outcomes
   c. Personnel accounting
   d. Ordering instructional materials

V. RESPONSIBILITIES OF THE SUPERVISOR

A person employed in a supervisory capacity must constantly be able to improve his own efficiency and ability. He represents the employer to the employees and only continuous self-examination can make him a capable supervisor.

Leadership and training are the supervisor's responsibility. An efficient working unit is one in which the employees work with the supervisor. It is his job to bring out the best in his employees. He must always be relaxed, courteous and calm in his association with his employees. Their feelings are important, and a harsh attitude does not develop the most efficient employees.

VI. COMPETENCIES OF THE SUPERVISOR

1. Complete knowledge of the duties and responsibilities of his position.
2. To be able to organize a job, plan ahead and carry through.
3. To have self-confidence and initiative.
4. To be able to handle the unexpected situation and make quick decisions.
5. To be able to properly train subordinates in the positions they are best suited for.
6. To be able to keep good human relations among his subordinates.
7. To be able to keep good human relations between his subordinates and himself and to earn their respect and trust.

VII. THE PROFESSIONAL SUPERVISOR-EMPLOYEE RELATIONSHIP

There are two kinds of efficiency: one kind is only apparent and is produced in organizations through the exercise of mere discipline; this is but a simulation of the second, or true, efficiency which springs from spontaneous cooperation. If you are a manager, no matter how great or small your responsibility, it is your job, in the final analysis, to create and develop this involuntary cooperation among the people whom you supervise. For, no matter how powerful a combination of money, machines, and materials a company may have, this is a dead and sterile thing without a team of willing, thinking and articulate people to guide it.

The following 21 points are presented as indicative of the exemplary basic relationship that should exist between supervisor and employee:

1. Each person wants to be liked and respected by his fellow employee and wants to be treated with consideration and respect by his superior.
2. The most competent employee will make an error. However, in a unit where good relations exist between the supervisor and his employees, tenseness and fear do not exist. Thus, errors are not hidden or covered up and the efficiency of a unit is not impaired.
3. Subordinates resent rules, regulations, or orders that are unreasonable or unexplained.
4. Subordinates are quick to resent unfairness, harshness, injustices and favoritism.
5. An employee will accept responsibility if he knows that he will be complimented for a job well done, and not too harshly chastised for failure; that his supervisor will check the cause of the failure, and, if it was the supervisor's fault, he will assume the blame therefore. If it was the employee's fault, his supervisor will explain the correct method or means of handling the responsibility.

6. An employee wants to receive credit for a suggestion he has made, that is used. If a suggestion cannot be used, the employee is entitled to an explanation. The supervisor should not say "no" and close the subject.
7. Fear and worry slow up a worker's ability. Poor working environment can impair his physical and mental health. A good supervisor avoids forceful methods, threats and arguments to get a job done.
8. A forceful supervisor is able to train his employees individually and as a team, and is able to motivate them in the proper channels.
9. A mature supervisor is able to properly evaluate his subordinates and to keep them happy and satisfied.
10. A sensitive supervisor will never patronize his subordinates.
11. A worthy supervisor will respect his employees' confidences.
12. Definite and clear-cut responsibilities should be assigned to each executive.
13. Responsibility should always be coupled with corresponding authority.
14. No change should be made in the scope or responsibilities of a position without a definite understanding to that effect on the part of all persons concerned.
15. No executive or employee, occupying a single position in the organization, should be subject to definite orders from more than one source.
16. Orders should never be given to subordinates over the head of a responsible executive. Rather than do this, the officer in question should be supplanted.
17. Criticisms of subordinates should, whoever possible, be made privately, and in no case should a subordinate be criticized in the presence of executives or employees of equal or lower rank.
18. No dispute or difference between executives or employees as to authority or responsibilities should be considered too trivial for prompt and careful adjudication.
19. Promotions, wage changes, and disciplinary action should always be approved by the executive immediately superior to the one directly responsible.
20. No executive or employee should ever be required, or expected, to be at the same time an assistant to, and critic of, another.
21. Any executive whose work is subject to regular inspection should, whever practicable, be given the assistance and facilities necessary to enable him to maintain an independent check of the quality of his work.

VIII. MINI-TEXT IN SUPERVISION, ADMINISTRATION, MANAGEMENT, AND ORGANIZATION

A. BRIEF HIGHLIGHTS

Listed concisely and sequentially are major headings and important data in the field for quick recall and review.

1. *LEVELS OF MANAGEMENT*

Any organization of some size has several levels of management. In terms of a ladder the levels are:

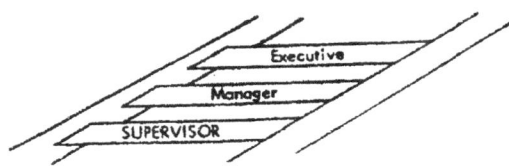

The first level is very important because it is the beginning point of management leadership.

2. WHAT THE SUPERVISOR MUST LEARN
A supervisor must learn to:
1. Deal with people and their differences
2. Get the job done through people
3. Recognize the problems when they exist
4. Overcome obstacles to good performance
5. Evaluate the performance of people
6. Check his own performance in terms of accomplishment

3. A DEFINITION OF SUPERVISOR
The term supervisor means any individual having authority, in the interests of the employer, to hire, transfer, suspend, lay-off, recall, promote, discharge, assign, reward, or discipline other employees or responsibility to direct them, or to adjust their grievances, or effectively to recommend such action, if, in connection with the foregoing, exercise of such authority is not of a merely routine or clerical nature but requires the use of independent judgment.

4. ELEMENTS OF THE TEAM CONCEPT
What is involved in teamwork? The component parts are:
1. Members
2. A leader
3. Goals
4. Plans
5. Cooperation
6. Spirit

5. PRINCIPLES OF ORGANIZATION
1. A team member must know what his job is.
2. Be sure that the nature and scope of a job are understood.
3. Authority and responsibility should be carefully spelled out.
4. A supervisor should be permitted to make the maximum number of decisions affecting his employees.
5. Employees should report to only one supervisor.
6. A supervisor should direct only as many employees as he can handle effectively.
7. An organization plan should be flexible.
8. Inspection and performance of work should be separate.
9. Organizational problems should receive immediate attention.
10. Assign work in line with ability and experience.

6. THE FOUR IMPORTANT PARTS OF EVERY JOB
1. Inherent in every job is the *accountability* for results.
2. A second set of factors in every job is *responsibilities.*
3. Along with duties and responsibilities one must have the *authority* to act within certain limits without obtaining permission to proceed.
4. No job exists in a vacuum. The supervisor is surrounded by key *relationships.*

7. PRINCIPLES OF DELEGATION
Where work is delegated for the first time, the supervisor should think in terms of these questions:
1. Who is best qualified to do this?
2. Can an employee improve his abilities by doing this?
3. How long should an employee spend on this?
4. Are there any special problems for which he will need guidance?
5. How broad a delegation can I make?

8. PRINCIPLES OF EFFECTIVE COMMUNICATIONS
   (1) Determine the media
   (2) To whom directed?
   (3) Identification and source authority
   (4) Is communication understood?

9. PRINCIPLES OF WORK IMPROVEMENT
   (1) Most people usually do only the work which is assigned to them
   (2) Workers are likely to fit assigned work into the time available to perform it
   (3) A good workload usually stimulates output
   (4) People usually do their best work when they know that results will be reviewed or inspected
   (5) Employees usually feel that someone else is responsible for conditions of work, workplace layout, job methods, type of tools/equipment, and other such factors
   (6) Employees are usually defensive about their job security
   (7) Employees have natural resistance to change
   (8) Employees can support or destroy a supervisor
   (9) A supervisor usually earns the respect of his people through his personal example of diligence and efficiency

10. AREAS OF JOB IMPROVEMENT
The areas of job improvement are quite numerous, but the most common ones which a supervisor can identify and utilize are:
   (1) Departmental layout
   (2) Flow of work
   (3) Workplace layout
   (4) Utilization of manpower
   (5) Work methods
   (6) Materials handling
   (7) Utilization
   (8) Motion economy

11. SEVEN KEY POINTS IN MAKING IMPROVEMENTS
   (1) Select the job to be improved
   (2) Study how it is being done now
   (3) Question the present method
   (4) Determine actions to be taken
   (5) Chart proposed method
   (6) Get approval and apply
   (7) Solicit worker participation

12. CORRECTIVE TECHNIQUES OF JOB IMPROVEMENT

Specific Problems	General Improvement	Corrective Techniques
(1) Size of workload	(1) Departmental layout	(1) Study with scale model
(2) Inability to meet schedules	(2) Flow of work	(2) Flow chart study
(3) Strain and fatigue	(3) Work plan layout	(3) Motion analysis
(4) Improper use of men and skills	(4) Utilization of manpower	(4) Comparison of units produced to standard allowance
(5) Waste, poor quality, unsafe conditions	(5) Work methods	(5) Methods analysis
(6) Bottleneck conditions that hinder output	(6) Materials handling	(6) Flow chart & equipment study
(7) Poor utilization of equipment and machine	(7) Utilization of equipment	(7) Down time vs. running time
(8) Efficiency and productivity of labor	(8) Motion economy	(8) Motion analysis

13. A PLANNING CHECKLIST
(1) Objectives
(2) Controls
(3) Delegations
(4) Communications
(5) Resources
(6) Resources
(7) Manpower
(8) Equipment
(9) Supplies and materials
(10) Utilization of time
(11) Safety
(12) Money
(13) Work
(14) Timing of improvements

14. FIVE CHARACTERISTICS OF GOOD DIRECTIONS
In order to get results, directions must be:
(1) Possible of accomplishment
(2) Agreeable with worker interests
(3) Related to mission
(4) Planned and complete
(5) Unmistakably clear

15. TYPES OF DIRECTIONS
(1) Demands or direct orders
(2) Requests
(3) Suggestion or implication
(4) Volunteering

16. CONTROLS
A typical listing of the overall areas in which the supervisor should establish controls might be:
(1) Manpower
(2) Materials
(3) Quality of work
(4) Quantity of work
(5) Time
(6) Space
(7) Money
(8) Methods

17. ORIENTING THE NEW EMPLOYEE
(1) Prepare for him
(2) Welcome the new employee
(3) Orientation for the job
(4) Follow-up

18. CHECKLIST FOR ORIENTING NEW EMPLOYEES

	Yes	No
(1) Do your appreciate the feelings of new employees when they first report for work?		
(2) Are you aware of the fact that the new employee must make a big adjustment to his job?		
(3) Have you given him good reasons for liking the job and the organization?		
(4) Have you prepared for his first day on the job?		
(5) Did you welcome him cordially and make him feel needed?		
(6) Did you establish rapport with him so that he feels free to talk and discuss matters with you?		
(7) Did you explain his job to him and his relationship to you?		
(8) Does he know that his work will be evaluated periodically on a basis that is fair and objective?		
(9) Did you introduce him to his fellow workers in such a way that they are likely to accept him?		
(10) Does he know what employee benefits he will receive?		
(11) Does he understand the importance of being on the job and what to do if he must leave his duty station?		
(12) Has he been impressed with the importance of accident prevention and safe practice?		
(13) Does he generally know his way around the department?		
(14) Is he under the guidance of a sponsor who will teach the right ways of doing things?		
(15) Do you plan to follow-up so that he will continue to adjust successfully to his job?		

19. *PRINCIPLES OF LEARNING*
    (1) Motivation   (2) Demonstration or explanation   (3) Practice

20. *CAUSES OF POOR PERFORMANCE*
    (1) Improper training for job
    (2) Wrong tools
    (3) Inadequate directions
    (4) Lack of supervisory follow-up
    (5) Poor communications
    (6) Lack of standards of performance
    (7) Wrong work habits
    (8) Low morale
    (9) Other

21. *FOUR MAJOR STEPS IN ON-THE-JOB INSTRUCTION*
    (1) Prepare the worker
    (2) Present the operation
    (3) Tryout performance
    (4) Follow-up

22. *EMPLOYEES WANT FIVE THINGS*
    (1) Security   (2) Opportunity   (3) Recognition   (4) Inclusion   (5) Expression

23. *SOME DON'TS IN REGARD TO PRAISE*
    (1) Don't praise a person for something he hasn't done
    (2) Don't praise a person unless you can be sincere
    (3) Don't be sparing in praise just because your superior withholds it from you
    (4) Don't let too much time elapse between good performance and recognition of it

24. *HOW TO GAIN YOUR WORKERS' CONFIDENCE*
    Methods of developing confidence include such things as:
    (1) Knowing the interests, habits, hobbies of employees
    (2) Admitting your own inadequacies
    (3) Sharing and telling of confidence in others
    (4) Supporting people when they are in trouble
    (5) Delegating matters that can be well handled
    (6) Being frank and straightforward about problems and working conditions
    (7) Encouraging others to bring their problems to you
    (8) Taking action on problems which impede worker progress

25. *SOURCES OF EMPLOYEE PROBLEMS*
    On-the-job causes might be such things as:
    (1) A feeling that favoritism is exercised in assignments
    (2) Assignment of overtime
    (3) An undue amount of supervision
    (4) Changing methods or systems
    (5) Stealing of ideas or trade secrets
    (6) Lack of interest in job
    (7) Threat of reduction in force
    (8) Ignorance or lack of communications
    (9) Poor equipment
    (10) Lack of knowing how supervisor feels toward employee
    (11) Shift assignments

    Off-the-job problems might have to do with:
    (1) Health   (2) Finances   (3) Housing   (4) Family

26. THE SUPERVISOR'S KEY TO DISCIPLINE

There are several key points about discipline which the supervisor should keep in mind:
  (1) Job discipline is one of the disciplines of life and is directed by the supervisor.
  (2) It is more important to correct an employee fault than to fix blame for it.
  (3) Employee performance is affected by problems both on the job and off.
  (4) Sudden or abrupt changes in behavior can be indications of important employee problems.
  (5) Problems should be dealt with as soon as possible after they are identified.
  (6) The attitude of the supervisor may have more to do with solving problems than the techniques of problem solving.
  (7) Correction of employee behavior should be resorted to only after the supervisor is sure that training or counseling will not be helpful.
  (8) Be sure to document your disciplinary actions.
  (9) Make sure that you are disciplining on the basis of facts rather than personal feelings.
  (10) Take each disciplinary step in order, being careful not to make snap judgments, or decisions based on impatience.

27. FIVE IMPORTANT PROCESSES OF MANAGEMENT

  (1) Planning   (2) Organizing   (3) Scheduling
  (4) Controlling (5) Motivating

28. WHEN THE SUPERVISOR FAILS TO PLAN

  (1) Supervisor creates impression of not knowing his job
  (2) May lead to excessive overtime
  (3) Job runs itself -- supervisor lacks control
  (4) Deadlines and appointments missed
  (5) Parts of the work go undone
  (6) Work interrupted by emergencies
  (7) Sets a bad example
  (8) Uneven workload creates peaks and valleys
  (9) Too much time on minor details at expense of more important tasks

29. FOURTEEN GENERAL PRINCIPLES OF MANAGEMENT

  (1) Division of work
  (2) Authority and responsibility
  (3) Discipline
  (4) Unity of command
  (5) Unity of direction
  (6) Subordination of individual interest to general interest
  (7) Remuneration of personnel
  (8) Centralization
  (9) Scalar chain
  (10) Order
  (11) Equity
  (12) Stability of tenure of personnel
  (13) Initiative
  (14) Esprit de corps

30. CHANGE

Bringing about change is perhaps attempted more often, and yet less well understood, than anything else the supervisor does. How do people generally react to change? (People tend to resist change that is imposed upon them by other individuals or circumstances.

Change is characteristic of every situation. It is a part of every real endeavor where the efforts of people are concerned.

A. Why do people resist change?
   People may resist change because of:
   (1) Fear of the unknown
   (2) Implied criticism
   (3) Unpleasant experiences in the past
   (4) Fear of loss of status
   (5) Threat to the ego
   (6) Fear of loss of economic stability

B. How can we best overcome the resistance to change?
   In initiating change, take these steps:
   (1) Get ready to sell
   (2) Identify sources of help
   (3) Anticipate objections
   (4) Sell benefits
   (5) Listen in depth
   (6) Follow up

B. BRIEF TOPICAL SUMMARIES

I. WHO/WHAT IS THE SUPERVISOR?
1. The supervisor is often called the "highest level employee and the lowest level manager."
2. A supervisor is a member of both management and the work group. He acts as a bridge between the two.
3. Most problems in supervision are in the area of human relations, or people problems.
4. Employees expect: Respect, opportunity to learn and to advance, and a sense of belonging, and so forth.
5. Supervisors are responsible for directing people and organizing work. Planning is of paramount importance.
6. A position description is a set of duties and responsibilities inherent to a given position.
7. It is important to keep the position description up-to-date and to provide each employee with his own copy.

II. THE SOCIOLOGY OF WORK
1. People are alike in many ways; however, each individual is unique.
2. The supervisor is challenged in getting to know employee differences. Acquiring skills in evaluating individuals is an asset.
3. Maintaining meaningful working relationships in the organization is of great importance.
4. The supervisor has an obligation to help individuals to develop to their fullest potential.
5. Job rotation on a planned basis helps to build versatility and to maintain interest and enthusiasm in work groups.
6. Cross training (job rotation) provides backup skills.
7. The supervisor can help reduce tension by maintaining a sense of humor, providing guidance to employees, and by making reasonable and timely decisions. Employees respond favorably to working under reasonably predictable circumstances.
8. Change is characteristic of all managerial behavior. The supervisor must adjust to changes in procedures, new methods, technological changes, and to a number of new and sometimes challenging situations.
9. To overcome the natural tendency for people to resist change, the supervisor should become more skillful in initiating change.

III. PRINCIPLES AND PRACTICES OF SUPERVISION

1. Employees should be required to answer to only one superior.
2. A supervisor can effectively direct only a limited number of employees, depending upon the complexity, variety, and proximity of the jobs involved.
3. The organizational chart presents the organization in graphic form. It reflects lines of authority and responsibility as well as interrelationships of units within the organization.
4. Distribution of work can be improved through an analysis using the "Work Distribution Chart."
5. The "Work Distribution Chart" reflects the division of work within a unit in understandable form.
6. When related tasks are given to an employee, he has a better chance of increasing his skills through training.
7. The individual who is given the responsibility for tasks must also be given the appropriate authority to insure adequate results.
8. The supervisor should delegate repetitive, routine work. Preparation of recurring reports, maintaining leave and attendance records are some examples.
9. Good discipline is essential to good task performance. Discipline is reflected in the actions of employees on the job in the absence of supervision.
10. Disciplinary action may have to be taken when the positive aspects of discipline have failed. Reprimand, warning, and suspension are examples of disciplinary action.
11. If a situation calls for a reprimand, be sure it is deserved and remember it is to be done in private.

IV. DYNAMIC LEADERSHIP

1. A style is a personal method or manner of exerting influence.
2. Authoritarian leaders often see themselves as the source of power and authority.
3. The democratic leader often perceives the group as the source of authority and power.
4. Supervisors tend to do better when using the pattern of leadership that is most natural for them.
5. Social scientists suggest that the effective supervisor use the leadership style that best fits the problem or circumstances involved.
6. All four styles -- telling, selling, consulting, joining -- have their place. Using one does not preclude using the other at another time.
7. The theory X point of view assumes that the average person dislikes work, will avoid it whenever possible, and must be coerced to achieve organizational objectives.
8. The theory Y point of view assumes that the average person considers work to be as natural as play, and, when the individual is committed, he requires little supervision or direction to accomplish desired objectives.
9. The leader's basic assumptions concerning human behavior and human nature affect his actions, decisions, and other managerial practices.
10. Dissatisfaction among employees is often present, but difficult to isolate. The supervisor should seek to weaken dissatisfaction by keeping promises, being sincere and considerate, keeping employees informed, and so forth.
11. Constructive suggestions should be encouraged during the natural progress of the work.

V. PROCESSES FOR SOLVING PROBLEMS

1. People find their daily tasks more meaningful and satisfying when they can improve them.
2. The causes of problems, or the key factors, are often hidden in the background. Ability to solve problems often involves the ability to isolate them from their backgrounds. There is some substance to the cliché that some persons "can't see the forest for the trees."
3. New procedures are often developed from old ones. Problems should be broken down into manageable parts. New ideas can be adapted from old ones.

4. People think differently in problem-solving situations. Using a logical, patterned approach is often useful. One approach found to be useful includes these steps:
   - (a) Define the problem
   - (b) Establish objectives
   - (c) Get the facts
   - (d) Weigh and decide
   - (e) Take action
   - (f) Evaluate action

VI. TRAINING FOR RESULTS
1. Participants respond best when they feel training is important to them.
2. The supervisor has responsibility for the training and development of those who report to him.
3. When training is delegated to others, great care must be exercised to insure the trainer has knowledge, aptitude, and interest for his work as a trainer.
4. Training (learning) of some type goes on continually. The most successful supervisor makes certain the learning contributes in a productive manner to operational goals.
5. New employees are particularly susceptible to training. Older employees facing new job situations require specific training, as well as having need for development and growth opportunities.
6. Training needs require continuous monitoring.
7. The training officer of an agency is a professional with a responsibility to assist supervisors in solving training problems.
8. Many of the self-development steps important to the supervisor's own growth are equally important to the development of peers and subordinates. Knowledge of these is important when the supervisor consults with others on development and growth opportunities.

VII. HEALTH, SAFETY, AND ACCIDENT PREVENTION
1. Management-minded supervisors take appropriate measures to assist employees in maintaining health and in assuring safe practices in the work environment.
2. Effective safety training and practices help to avoid injury and accidents.
3. Safety should be a management goal. All infractions of safety which are observed should be corrected without exception.
4. Employees' safety attitude, training and instruction, provision of safe tools and equipment, supervision, and leadership are considered highly important factors which contribute to safety and which can be influenced directly by supervisors.
5. When accidents do occur they should be investigated promptly for very important reasons, including the fact that information which is gained can be used to prevent accidents in the future.

VIII. EQUAL EMPLOYMENT OPPORTUNITY
1. The supervisor should endeavor to treat all employees fairly, without regard to religion, race, sex, or national origin.
2. Groups tend to reflect the attitude of the leader. Prejudice can be detected even in very subtle form. Supervisors must strive to create a feeling of mutual respect and confidence in every employee.
3. Complete utilization of all human resources is a national goal. Equitable consideration should be accorded women in the work force, minority-group members, the physically and mentally handicapped, and the older employee. The important question is: "Who can do the job?"
4. Training opportunities, recognition for performance, overtime assignments, promotional opportunities, and all other personnel actions are to be handled on an equitable basis.

IX. IMPROVING COMMUNICATIONS

1. Communications is achieving understanding between the sender and the receiver of a message. It also means sharing information -- the creation of understanding.
2. Communication is basic to all human activity. Words are means of conveying meanings; however, real meanings are in people.
3. There are very practical differences in the effectiveness of one-way, impersonal, and two-way communications. Words spoken face-to-face are better understood. Telephone conversations are effective, but lack the rapport of person-to-person exchanges. The whole person communicates.
4. Cooperation and communication in an organization go hand in hand. When there is a mutual respect between people, spelling out rules and procedures for communicating is unnecessary.
5. There are several barriers to effective communications. These include failure to listen with respect and understanding, lack of skill in feedback, and misinterpreting the meanings of words used by the speaker. It is also common practice to listen to what we want to hear, and tune out things we do not want to hear.
6. Communication is management's chief problem. The supervisor should accept the challenge to communicate more effectively and to improve interagency and intra-agency communications.
7. The supervisor may often plan for and conduct meetings. The planning phase is critical and may determine the success or the failure of a meeting.
8. Speaking before groups usually requires extra effort. Stage fright may never disappear completely, but it can be controlled.

X. SELF-DEVELOPMENT

1. Every employee is responsible for his own self-development.
2. Toastmaster and toastmistress clubs offer opportunities to improve skills in oral communications.
3. Planning for one's own self-development is of vital importance. Supervisors know their own strengths and limitations better than anyone else.
4. Many opportunities are open to aid the supervisor in his developmental efforts, including job assignments; training opportunities, both governmental and non-governmental -- to include universities and professional conferences and seminars.
5. Programmed instruction offers a means of studying at one's own rate.
6. Where difficulties may arise from a supervisor's being away from his work for training, he may participate in televised home study or correspondence courses to meet his self-develop- ment needs.

XI. TEACHING AND TRAINING

A. The Teaching Process

Teaching is encouraging and guiding the learning activities of students toward established goals. In most cases this process consists in five steps: preparation, presentation, summarization, evaluation, and application.

1. Preparation

    Preparation is twofold in nature; that of the supervisor and the employee.
    Preparation by the supervisor is absolutely essential to success. He must know what, when, where, how, and whom he will teach. Some of the factors that should be considered are:

    (1) The objectives
    (2) The materials needed
    (3) The methods to be used
    (4) Employee participation
    (5) Employee interest
    (6) Training aids
    (7) Evaluation
    (8) Summarization

Employee preparation consists in preparing the employee to receive the material. Probably the most important single factor in the preparation of the employee is arousing and maintaining his interest. He must know the objectives of the training, why he is there, how the material can be used, and its importance to him.

2. Presentation

In presentation, have a carefully designed plan and follow it.
The plan should be accurate and complete, yet flexible enough to meet situations as they arise. The method of presentation will be determined by the particular situation and objectives.

3. Summary

A summary should be made at the end of every training unit and program. In addition, there may be internal summaries depending on the nature of the material being taught. The important thing is that the trainee must always be able to understand how each part of the new material relates to the whole.

4. Application

The supervisor must arrange work so the employee will be given a chance to apply new knowledge or skills while the material is still clear in his mind and interest is high. The trainee does not really know whether he has learned the material until he has been given a chance to apply it. If the material is not applied, it loses most of its value.

5. Evaluation

The purpose of all training is to promote learning. To determine whether the training has been a success or failure, the supervisor must evaluate this learning.

In the broadest sense evaluation includes all the devices, methods, skills, and techniques used by the supervisor to keep him self and the employees informed as to their progress toward the objectives they are pursuing. The extent to which the employee has mastered the knowledge, skills, and abilities, or changed his attitudes, as determined by the program objectives, is the extent to which instruction has succeeded or failed.

Evaluation should not be confined to the end of the lesson, day, or program but should be used continuously. We shall note later the way this relates to the rest of the teaching process.

B. Teaching Methods

A teaching method is a pattern of identifiable student and instructor activity used in presenting training material.
All supervisors are faced with the problem of deciding which method should be used at a given time.
As with all methods, there are certain advantages and disadvantages to each method.

1. Lecture

The lecture is direct oral presentation of material by the supervisor. The present trend is to place less emphasis on the trainer's activity and more on that of the trainee.

2. Discussion

Teaching by discussion or conference involves using questions and other techniques to arouse interest and focus attention upon certain areas, and by doing so creating a learning situation. This can be one of the most valuable methods because it gives the employees 'an opportunity to express their ideas and pool their knowledge.

3. Demonstration

The demonstration is used to teach how something works or how to do something. It can be used to show a principle or what the results of a series of actions will be. A well-staged demonstration is particularly effective because it shows proper methods of performance in a realistic manner.

4. Performance

Performance is one of the most fundamental of all learning techniques or teaching methods. The trainee may be able to tell how a specific operation should be performed but he cannot be sure he knows how to perform the operation until he has done so.

5. Which Method to Use

Moreover, there are other methods and techniques of teaching. It is difficult to use any method without other methods entering into it. In any learning situation a combination of methods is usually more effective than anyone method alone.

Finally, evaluation must be integrated into the other aspects of the teaching-learning process.
It must be used in the motivation of the trainees; it must be used to assist in developing understanding during the training; and it must be related to employee application of the results of training.

This is distinctly the role of the supervisor.

GLOSSARY OF REAL ESTATE TERMS

TABLE OF CONTENTS

	Page
Abstract of Title ... Alienation	1
Amortization ... Avulsion	2
Beneficiary ... Cease and Desist Order	3
Cease and Desist Petition ... Conversion	4
Conveyance ... Depreciation	5
Descent ... Equity	6
Equity of Redemption ... Exclusive Right to Sell	7
Executor ... Gross Lease	8
Ground Rent ... Jeopardy	9
Joint Tenancy ... Mandatory	10
Market Value ... Multiple Listing	11
Net Listing ... Personal Property	12
Plat Book ... Recording	13
Redemption ... Set Back	14
Severalty ... Tenancy at Will	15
Tenant ... Voidable	16
Waiver ... Zoning Ordinance	17

GLOSSARY OF REAL ESTATE TERMS

A

Abstract of Title - A summary of all of the recorded instruments and proceedings which affect the title to property, arranged in chronological order.

Accretion - The addition to land through processes of nature, as by streams or wind.

Accrued Interest - Accrue: to grow; to be added to. Accrued interest is interest that has been earned but not due and payable.

Acknowledgment - A formal declaration before a duly authorized officer by a person who has executed an instrument that such execution is the person's act and deed.

Acquisition- An act or process by which a person procures property.

Acre - A measure of land equaling 160 square rods or 4,840 square yards or 43,560 feet.

Adjacent - Lying near to but not necessarily in actual contact with.

Adjoining - Contiguous; attaching, in actual contact with.

Administrator - A person appointed by court to administer the estate of a deceased person who left no will; i.e., who died intestate.

Ad Valorem - According to valuation.

Adverse Possession - A means of acquiring title where an occupant has been in actual, open, notorious, exclusive, and continuous occupancy of property under a claim of right for the required statutory period.

Affidavit - A statement or declaration reduced to writing, and sworn to or affirmed before some officer who is authorized to administer an oath or affirmation.

Affirm - To confirm, to ratify, to verify.

Agency - That relationship between principal and agent which arises out of a contract either expressed or implied, written or oral, wherein an agent is employed by a person to do certain acts on the person's behalf in dealing with a third party.

Agent - One who undertakes to transact some business or to manage some affair for another by authority of the latter.

Agreement of Sale - A written agreement between seller and purchaser in which the purchaser agrees to buy certain real estate and the seller agrees to sell upon terms and conditions set forth therein.

Alienation - A transferring of property to another; the transfer of property and possession of lands, or other things, from one person to another.

Amortization - A gradual paying off of a debt by periodical installments.

Apportionments - Adjustment of the income, expenses or carrying charges of real estate usually computed to the date of closing of title so that the seller pays all expenses to that date. The buyer assumes all expenses commencing the date the deed is conveyed to the buyer.

Appraisal - An estimate of a property's valuation by an appraiser who is usually presumed to be expert in this work.

Appraisal by Capitalization - An estimate of value by capitalization of productivity and income.

Appraisal by Comparison - Comparability with the sale prices of other similar properties.

Appraisal by Summation - Adding together all parts of a property separately appraised to form a whole: e.g., value of the land considered as vacant added to the cost of reproduction of the building, less depreciation.

Appurtenance - Something which is outside the property itself but belongs to the land and adds to its greater enjoyment such as a right of way or a barn or a dwelling.

Assessed Valuation - A valuation placed upon property by a public officer or a board, as a basis for taxation.

Assessment - A charge against real estate made by a unit of government to cover a proportionate cost of an improvement such as a street or sewer.

Assessor - An official who has the responsibility of determining assessed values.

Assignee - The person to whom an agreement or contract is assigned.

Assignment - The method or manner by which a right, a specialty, or contract is transferred from one person to another.

Assignor - A party who assigns or transfers an agreement or contract to another.

Assumption of Mortgage - The taking of title to property by a grantee, wherein the grantee assumes liability for payment of an existing note or bond secured by a mortgage against a property and becomes personally liable for the payment of such mortgage debt.

Attest - To witness to; to witness by observation and signature.

Avulsion - The removal of land from one owner to another, when a stream suddenly changes its channel.

B

Beneficiary - The person who receives or is to receive the benefits resulting from certain acts.

Bequeath - To give or hand down by will; to leave by will.

Bequest - That which is given by the terms of a will.

Bill of Sale - A written instrument given to pass title of personal property from vendor to vendee.

Binder - An agreement to cover the down payment for the purchase of real estate as evidence of good faith on the part of the purchaser.

Blanket Mortgage - A single mortgage which covers more than one piece of real estate.

Bona Fide - In good faith, without fraud.

Bond - The evidence of a personal debt which is secured by a mortgage or other lien on real estate.

Building Codes - Regulations established by local governments stating fully the structural requirements for building.

Building Line - A line fixed at a certain distance from the front and/or sides of a lot, beyond which no building can project.

Building Loan Agreement - An agreement whereby the lender advances money to an owner with provisional payments at certain stages of construction.

C

Cancellation Clause - A provision in a lease which confers upon One or more or all of the parties to the lease the right to terminate the party's or parties' obligations thereunder upon the occurrence of the condition or contingency set forth in the said clause.

Caveat Emptor - Let the buyer beware. The buyer must examine the goods or property and buy at the buyer's own risk.

Cease and Desist Order - An order executed by the Secretary of State directing broker recipients to cease and desist from all solicitation of homeowners whose names and addresses appear on the list(s) forwarded with such order.
The order acknowledges petition filings by homeowners listed evidencing their premises are not for sale, thereby revoking the implied invitation to solicit.
The issuance of a Cease and Desist Order does not prevent an owner from selling or listing his premises for sale. It prohibits soliciting by licensees served with such order and subjects violators to penalties of suspension or revocation of their licenses as provided in section 441-c of the Real Property Law.

Cease and Desist Petition - A statement filed by a homeowner showing address of premises owned which notifies the Department of State that such premises are not for sale and does not wish to be solicited. In so doing, petitioner revokes the implied invitation to be solicited, by any means with respect thereto, by licensed real estate brokers and salespersons.

Certiorari - A proceeding to review in a competent court the action of an inferior tribunal board or officer exercising judicial functions.

Chain of Title - A history of conveyances and encumbrances affecting a title from the time the original patent was granted, or as far back as records are available.

Chattel - Personal property, such as household goods or fixtures.

Chattel Mortgage - A mortgage on personal property.

Client - The one by whom a broker is employed and by whom the broker will be compensated on completion of the purpose of the agency.

Closing Date - The date upon which the buyer takes over the property; usually between 30 and 60 days after the signing of the contract.

Cloud on the Title - An outstanding claim or encumbrance which, if valid, would affect or impair the owner's title.

Collateral - Additional security pledged for the payment of an obligation.

Color of Title - That which appears to be good title, but which is not title in fact.

Commission - A sum due a real estate broker for services in that capacity.

Commitment - A pledge or a promise or affirmation agreement.

Condemnation - Taking private property for public use, with fair compensation to the owner; exercising the right of eminent domain.

Conditional Sales Contract - A contract for the sale of property stating that delivery is to be made to the buyer, title to remain vested in the seller until the conditions of the contract have been fulfilled.

Consideration - Anything of value given to induce entering into a contract; it may be money, personal services, or even love and affection.

Constructive Notice - Information or knowledge of a fact imputed by law to a person because the person could have discovered the fact by proper diligence and inquiry; (public records).

Contract - An agreement between competent parties to do or not to do certain things for a legal consideration, whereby each party acquires a right to what the other possesses.

Conversion - Change from one character or use to another.

Conveyance - The transfer of the title of land from one to another. The means or medium by which title of real estate is transferred.

County Clerk's Certificate - When an acknowledgment is taken by an officer not authorized in the state or county where the document is to be recorded, the instrument which must be attached to the acknowledgment is called a county clerk's certificate. It is given by the clerk of the county where the officer obtained his/her authority and certifies to the officer's signature and powers.

Covenants - Agreements written into deeds and other instruments promising performance or nonperformance of certain acts, or stipulating certain uses or nonuses of the property.

D

Damages - The indemnity recoverable by a person who has sustained an injury, either to his/her person, property or relative rights, through the art or default of another.

Decedent - One who is dead.

Decree - Order issued by one in authority; an edirt or law; a judicial decision.

Dedication - A grant and appropriation of land by its owner for some public use, accepted for such use, by an authorized public official on behalf of the public.

Deed - An instrument in writing duly executed and delivered, that conveys title to real property.

Deed Restriction - An imposed restriction in a deed for the purpose of limiting the use of the land such as:
1. A restriction against the sale of liquor thereon.
2. A restriction as to the size, type, value or placement of improvements that may be erected thereon.

Default - Failure to fulfill a duty or promise, or to discharge an obligation; omission or failure to perform any acts.

Defendant - The party sued or called to answer in any suit, civil or criminal, at law or in equity.

Deficiency Judgment - A judgment given when the security for a loan does not entirely satisfy the debt upon its default.

Delivery - The transfer of the possession of a thing from one person to another.

Demising Clause - A clause found in a lease whereby the landlord (lessor) leases and the tenant (lessee) takes the property.

Depreciation - Loss of value in real property brought about by age, physical deterioration, or functional or economic obsolescence.

Descent - When an owner of real estate dies intestate, the owner's property descends, by operation of law, to the owner's distributees.

Devise - A gift of real estate by will or last testament.

Devisee - One who receives a bequest of real estate made by will.

Devisor - One who bequeaths real estate by will.

Directional Growth - The location or direction toward which the residential sections of a city are destined or determined to grow.

Dispossess Proceedings - Summary process by a landlord to oust a tenant and regain possession of the premises for nonpayment of rent or other breach of conditions of the lease or occupancy.

Distributee - Person receiving or entitled to receive land as representative of the former owner.

Documentary Evidence - Evidence in the form of written or printed papers.

Duress - Unlawful constraint exercised upon a person whereby the person is forced to do some act against his will.

E

Earnest Money - Down payment made by a purchaser of real estate as evidence of good faith.

Easement - A right that may be exercised by the public or individuals on, over or through the lands of others.

Ejectment - A form of action to regain possession of real property, with damages for the unlawful retention; used when there is no relationship of landlord and tenant.

Eminent Domain - A right of the government to acquire property for necessary public use by condemnation; the owner must be fairly compensated.

Encroachment - A building, part of a building, or obstruction which intrudes upon or invades a highway or sidewalk or trespasses upon the property of another.

Encumbrance - Any right to or interest in land that diminishes its value. *(Also Incumbrance)*

Endorsement - An act of signing one's name on the back of a check or note, with or without further qualifications.

Equity - The interest or value which the owner has in real estate over and above the liens against it.

Equity of Redemption - A right of the owner to reclaim property before it is sold through foreclosure proceedings, by the payment of the debt, interest and costs.

Erosion - The wearing away of land through processes of nature, as by streams and winds.

Escheat - The reversion to the state of property in event the owner thereof dies, without leaving a will and has no distributees to whom the property may pass by lawful descent.

Escrow - A written agreement between two or more parties providing that certain instruments or property be placed with a third party to be delivered to a designated person upon the fulfillment or performance of some act or condition.

Estate - The degree, quantity, nature and extent of interest which a person has in real property.

Estate for Life - An estate or interest held during the terms of some certain person's life.

Estate in Reversion - The residue of an estate left for the grantor, to commence in possession after the termination of some particular estate granted by the grantor.

Estate at Will - The occupation of lands and tenements by a tenant for an indefinite period, terminable by one or both parties at will.

Estoppel Certificate - An instrument executed by the mortgagor setting forth the present status and the balance due on the mortgage as of the date of the execution of the certificate.

Eviction - A legal proceeding by a lessor landlord to recover possession of real property.

Eviction, Actual - Where one is, either by force or by process of law, actually put out of possession.

Eviction, Constructive - Any disturbance of the tenant's possessions by the landlord whereby the premises are rendered unfit or unsuitable for the purpose for which they were leased.

Eviction, Partial - Where the possessor of the premises is deprived of a portion thereof.

Exclusive Agency - An agreement of employment of a broker to the exclusion of all other brokers; if sale is made by any other broker during term of employment, broker holding exclusive agency is entitled to commissions in addition to the commissions payable to the broker who effected the transaction.

Exclusive Right to Sell - An agreement of employment by a broker under which the exclusive right to sell for a specified period is granted to the broker; if a sale during the term of the agreement is made by the owner or by any other broker, the broker holding such exclusive right to sell is nevertheless entitled to compensation.

Executor - A male person or a corporate entity or any other type of organization named or designated in a will to carry out its provisions as to the disposition of the estate of a deceased person.

Executrix - A woman appointed to perform the duties similar to those of an executor.

Extension Agreement - An agreement which extends the life of a mortgage to a later date.

F

Fee; Fee Simple; Fee Absolute - Absolute ownership of real property; a person has this type of estate where the person is entitled to the entire property with unconditional power of disposition during the person's life and descending to the person's distributees and legal representatives upon the person's death intestate.

Fiduciary - A person who on behalf of or for the benefit of another transacts business or handles money on property not the person's own; such relationship implies great confidence and trust.

Fixtures - Personal property so attached to the land or improvements as to become part of the real property.

Foreclosure - A procedure whereby property pledged as security for a debt is sold to pay the debt in the event of default in payments or terms.

Forfeiture - Loss of money or anything of value, by way of penalty due to failure to perform.

Freehold - An interest in real estate, not less than an estate for life. (Use of this term discontinued Sept. 1, 1967.)

Front Foot - A standard measurement, one foot wide, of the width of land, applied at the frontage on its street line. Each front foot extends the depth of the lot.

G

Grace Period - Additional time allowed to perform an act or make a payment before a default occurs.

Graduated Leases - A lease which provides for a graduated change at stated intervals in the amount of the rent to be paid; used largely in long term leases.

Grant - A technical term used in deeds of conveyance of lands to indicate a transfer.

Grantee - The party to whom the title to real property is conveyed.

Grantor - The person who conveys real estate by deed; the seller.

Gross Income - Total income from property before any expenses are deducted.

Gross Lease - A lease of property whereby the lessor is to meet all property charges regularly incurred through ownership.

Ground Rent - Earnings of improved property credited to earning of the ground itself after allowance made for earnings of improvements.

H

Habendum Clause - The "To Have and To Hold" clause which defines or limits the quantity of the estate granted in the premises of the deed.

Hereditaments - The largest classification of property; including lands, tenements and incorporeal property, such as rights of way.

Holdover Tenant - A tenant who remains in possession of leased property after the expiration of the lease term.

Hypothecate - To give a thing as security without the necessity of giving up possession of it.

I

In Rem - A proceeding against the realty directly; as distinguished from a proceeding against a person. (Used in taking land for nonpayment of taxes, etc.)

Incompetent - A person who is unable to manage his/her own affairs by reason of insanity, inbecility or feeble-mindedness.

Incumbrance - Any right to or interest in land that diminishes its value. *(Also Encumbrance)*

Injunction - A writ or order issued under the seal of a court to restrain one or more parties to a suit or proceeding from doing an act which is deemed to be inequitable or unjust in regard to the rights of some other party or parties in the suit or proceeding.

Installments - Parts of the same debt, payable at successive periods as agreed; payments made to reduce a mortgage.

Instrument - A written legal document; created to effect the rights of the parties.

Interest Rate - The percentage of a sum of money charged for its use.

Intestate - A person who dies having made no will, or leaves one which is defective in form, in which case the person's estate descends to the person's distributees.

Involuntary Lien - A lien imposed against property without consent of the owner, i.e., taxes, special assessments.

Irrevocable - Incapable of being recalled or revoked; unchangeable; unalterable.

J

Jeopardy - Peril, danger.

Joint Tenancy - Ownership of realty by two or more persons, each of whom has an undivided interest with the "right of survivorship."

Judgment - Decree of a court declaring that one individual is indebted to another, and fixing the amount of such indebtedness.

Junior Mortgage - A mortgage second in lien to a previous mortgage.

L

Laches - Delay or negligence in asserting one's legal rights.

Land, Tenements and Hereditaments - A phrase used in the early English Law, to express all sorts of property of the immovable class.

Landlord - One who rents property to another.

Lease - A contract whereby, for a consideration, usually termed rent, one who is entitled to the possession of real property transfers such rights to another for life, for a term of years, or at will.

Leasehold - The interest or estate which a lessee of real estate has therein by virtue of the lessee's lease.

Lessee - A person to whom property is rented under a lease.

Lessor - One who rents property to another under a lease.

Lien - A legal right or claim upon a specific property which attaches to the property until a debt is satisfied.

Lien (Mechanic's) - A notice filed with the County Clerk stating that payment has not been made for an improvement to real property.

Life Estate - The conveyance of title to property for the duration of the life of the grantee.

Life Tenant - The holder of a life estate.

Lis Pendens - A legal document, filed in the office of the county clerk giving notice that an action or proceeding is pending in the courts affecting the title to the property.

Listing - An employment contract between principal and agent, authorizing the agent to perform services for the principal involving the latter's property.

Litigation - The act of carrying on a lawsuit.

M

Mandatory - Requiring strict conformity or obedience.

Market Value - The highest price which a buyer, willing but not compelled to buy, would pay, and the lowest a seller, willing but not compelled to sell, would accept.

Marketable Title - A title which a court of equity considers to be so free from defect that it will enforce its acceptance by a purchaser.

Mechanic's Lien - A lien given by law upon a building or other improvement upon land, and upon the land itself, to secure the price of labor done upon, and materials furnished for. the improvement.

Meeting of the Minds - Whenever all parties to a contract agree to the exact terms thereof.

Metes and Bounds - A term used in describing the boundary lines of land, setting forth all the boundary lines together with their terminal points and angles.

Minor - A person under an age specified by law; under 18 years of age.

Monument - A fixed object and point established by surveyors to establish land locations.

Moratorium - An emergency act by a legislative body to suspend the legal enforcement of contractual obligations.

Mortgage - An instrument in writing, duly executed and delivered, that creates a lien upon real estate as security for the payment of a specified debt, which is usually in the form of a bond.

Mortgage Commitment - A formal indication, by a lending institution that it will grant a mortgage loan on property, in a certain specified amount and on certain specified terms.

Mortgage Reduction Certificate - An instrument executed by the mortgagee, setting forth the present status and the balance due on the mortgage as of the date of the execution of the instrument.

Mortgagee - The party who lends money and takes a mortgage to secure the payment thereof.

Mortgagor - A person who borrows money and gives a mortgage on the person's property as security for the payment of the debt.

Multiple Listing - An arrangement among Real Estate Board of Exchange Members, whereby each broker presents the broker's listings to the attention of the other members so that if a sale results, the commission is divided between the broker bringing the listing and the broker making the sale.

N

Net Listing - A price below which an owner will not sell the property, and at which price a broker will not receive a commission; the broker receives the excess over and above the net listing as the broker's commission.

Notary Public - A public officer who is authorized to take acknowledgments to certain classes of documents, such as deeds, contracts, mortgages, and before whom affidavits may be sworn.

O

Obligee - The person in whose favor an obligation is entered into.

Obligor - The person who binds himself/herself to another; one who has engaged to perform some obligation; one who makes a bond.

Obsolescence - Loss in value due to reduced desirability and usefulness of a structure because its design and construction become obsolete; loss because of becoming old-fashioned, and not in keeping with modern means, with consequent loss of income.

Open End Mortgage - A mortgage under which the mortgagor may secure additional funds from the mortgagee, usually up to but not exceeding the original amount of the existing amortizing mortgage.

Open Listing - A listing given to any number of brokers without liability to compensate any except the one who first secures a buyer ready, willing and able to meet the terms of the listing, or secures the acceptance by the seller of a satisfactory offer; the sale of the property automatically terminates the listing.

Open Mortgage - A mortgage that has matured or is overdue and, therefore, is "open" to foreclosure at any time.

Option - A right given for a consideration to purchase or lease a property upon specified terms within a specified time; if the right is not exercised the option holder is not subject to liability for damages; if exercised, the grantor of option must perform.

P

Partition - The division which is made of real property between those who own it in undivided shares.

Party Wall - A party wall is a wall built along the line separating two properties, partly on each, which wall either owner, the owner's heirs and assigns has the right to use; such right constituting an easement over so much of the adjoining owner's land as is covered by the wall.

Percentage Lease - A lease of property in which the rental is based upon the percentage of the volume of sales made upon the leased premises, usually provides for minimum rental.

Personal Property - Any property which is not real property.

Plat Book - A public record containing maps of land showing the division of such land into streets, blocks and lots and indicating the measurements of the individual parcels.

Plottage - Increment in unity value of a plot of land created by assembling smaller ownerships into one ownership.

Police Power - The right of any political body to enact laws and enforce them, for the order, safety, health, morals and general welfare of the public.

Power of Attorney - A written instrument duly signed and executed by an owner of property, which authorizes an agent to act on behalf of the owner to the extent indicated in the instrument.

Premises - Lands and tenements; an estate; the subject matter of a conveyance.

Prepayment Clause - A clause in a mortgage which gives a mortgagor the privilege of paying the mortgage indebtedness before it becomes due.

Principal - The employer of an agent or broker; the broker's or agent's client.

Probate - To establish the will of a deceased person.

Purchase Money Mortgage - A mortgage given by a grantee in part payment of the purchase price of real estate.

Q

Quiet Enjoyment - The right of an owner or a person legally in possession to the use of property without interference of possession.

Quiet Title Suit - A suit in court to remove a defect, cloud or suspicion regarding legal rights of an owner to a certain parcel of real property.

Quitclaim Deed - A deed which conveys simply the grantor's rights or interest in real estate, without any agreement or covenant as to the nature or extent of that interest, or any other covenants; usually used to remove a cloud from the title.

R

Real Estate Board - An organization whose members consist primarily of real estate brokers and salespersons.

Real Property - Land, and generally whatever is erected upon or affixed thereto.

Realtor - A coined word which may only be used by an active member of a local real estate board, affiliated with the National Association of Real Estate Boards.

Recording - The act of writing or entering in a book of public record instruments affecting the title to real property.

Redemption - The right of a mortgagor to redeem the property by paying a debt after the expiration date and before sale at foreclosure; the right of an owner to reclaim the owner's property after the sale for taxes.

Release - The act or writing by which some claim or interest is surrendered to another.

Release Clause - A clause found in a blanket mortgage which gives the owner of the property the privilege of paying off a portion of the mortgage indebtedness, and thus freeing a portion of the property from the mortgage.

Rem - *(See In Rem)*

Remainder - An estate which takes effect after the termination of a prior estate such as a life estate.

Remainderman - The person who is to receive the property after the death of a life tenant.

Rent - The compensation paid for the use of real estate.

Reproduction Cost - Normal cost of exact duplication of a property as of a certain date.

Restriction - A limitation placed upon the use of property contained in the deed or other written instrument in the chain of title.

Reversionary Interest - The interest which a person has in lands or other property upon the termination of the preceding estate.

Revocation - An act of recalling a power of authority conferred, as the revocation of a power of attorney, a license, an agency, etc.

Right of Survivorship - Right of the surviving joint owner to succeed to the interests of the deceased joint owner, distinguishing feature of a joint tenancy or tenancy by the entirety.

Right of Way - The right to pass over another's land more or less frequently according to the nature of the easement.

Riparian Owner - One who owns land bounding upon a river or watercourse.

Riparian Rights - The right of a landowner to water on, under or adjacent to his land.

S

Sales Contract - A contract by which the buyer and seller agree to terms of sale.

Satisfaction Piece - An instrument for recording and acknowledging payment of an indebtedness secured by a mortgage.

Seizin - The possession of land by one who claims to own at least an estate for life therein.

Set Back - The distance from the curb or other established line, within which no buildings may be erected.

Severalty - The ownership of real property by an individual, as an individual.

Special Assessment - An assessment made against a property to pay for a public improvement by which the assessed property is supposed to be especially benefited.

Specific Performance - A remedy in a court of equity compelling a defendant to carry out the terms of an agreement or contract.

Statute - A law established by an act of the Legislature.

Statute of Frauds - State law which provides that certain contracts must be in writing in order to be enforceable at law.

Stipulations - The terms within a written contract.

Straight Line Depreciation - A definite sum set aside annually from income to pay costs of replacing improvements, without reference to the interest it earns.

Subdivision - A tract of land divided into lots or plots suitable for home building purposes.

Subletting - A leasing by a tenant to another, who holds under the tenant.

Subordination Clause - A clause which permits the placing of a mortgage at a later date which takes priority over an existing mortgage.

Subscribing Witness - One who writes his/her name as witness to the execution of an instrument.

Surety - One who guarantees the performance of another; guarantor.

Surrender -The cancellation of a lease by mutual consent of the lessor and the lessee.

Surrogate's Court (Probate Court) - A court having jurisdiction over the proof of wills, the settling of estates and of citations.

Survey - The process by which a parcel of land is measured and its area ascertained; also the blueprint showing the measurements, boundaries and area.

T

Tax Sale - Sale of property after a period of nonpayment of taxes.

Tenancy in Common - An ownership of realty by two or more persons, each of whom has an undivided interest, without the "right of survivorship."

Tenancy by the Entirety - An estate which exists only between husband and wife with equal right of possession and enjoyment during their joint lives and with the "right of survivorship."

Tenancy at Will - A license to use or occupy lands and tenements at the will of the owner.

Tenant - One who is given possession of real estate for a fixed period or at will.

Tenant at Sufferance - One who comes into possession of lands by lawful title and keeps it afterwards without any title at all.

Testate - Where a person dies leaving a valid will.

Title - Evidence that owner of land is in lawful possession thereof; evidence of ownership.

Title Insurance - A policy of insurance which indemnifies the holder for any loss sustained by reason of defects in the title.

Title Search - An examination of the public records to determine the ownership and encumbrances affecting real property.

Torrens Title - System of title records provided by state law; it is a system for the registration of land titles whereby the state of the title, showing ownership and encumbrances, can be readily ascertained from an inspection of the "register of titles" without the necessity of a search of the public records.

Tort - A wrongful act, wrong, injury; violation of a legal right.

Transfer Tax - A tax charged under certain conditions on the properly belonging to an estate.

U

Unearned Increment - An increase in value of real estate due to no effort on the part of the owner: often due to increase in population.

Urban Property - City property; closely settled property.

Usury - On a loan, claiming a rate of interest greater than that permitted by law.

V

Valid - Having force, or binding force; legally sufficient and authorized by law.

Valuation - Estimated worth or price. The art of valuing by appraisal.

Vendee's Lien - A lien against property under contract of sale to secure deposit paid by a purchaser.

Verification - Sworn statements before a duly qualified officer to the correctness of the contents of an instrument.

Violations - Act, deed or conditions contrary to law or permissible use of real property.

Void - To have no force or effect; that which is unenforceable.

Voidable - That which is capable of being adjudged void, but is not void unless action is taken to make it so.

W

Waiver - The renunciation, abandonment or surrender of some claim, right or privilege.

Warranty Deed - A conveyance of land in which the grantor warrants the title to the grantee.

Will - The disposition of one's property to take effect after death.

Without - RecourseWords used in endorsing a note or bill to denote that the future holder is not co look to the endorser in case of nonpayment.

Z

Zone - An area set off by the proper authorities for specific use; subject to certain restrictions or restraints.

Zoning Ordinance - Act of city or county or other authorities specifying type and use to which property may be put in specific areas.

Made in the USA
Middletown, DE
02 December 2020